Common Core Writing Handbook

GRADE

2

HOUGHTON MIFFLIN HARCOURT

Contents

Contents

Writing Models and Forms

How to Use This Book

This handbook will help you learn to write better. It will give you ideas and tips. It will also help you share your ideas.

What Is a Handbook?

A handbook is a special tool for writing. First, you read about how to write. Then you practice writing.

You can use the pages in this book over and over again. Any time that you have a writing question, use this book.

Parts of This Book

This handbook has three parts:

1. **Writing Forms**—Examples of different kinds of writing

2. **Writing Strategies**—Ideas and steps that you can use for writing

3. **Writing Models and Forms**—Examples of good writing

Enjoy using this handbook!

Purposes for Writing

One of the first things you should think about before you write is your purpose, or reason for writing.

● To Inform

To inform is to tell facts and details about a person, place, or thing. Some kinds of writing that inform are reports, informative paragraphs, and instructions.

● To Explain

To explain means to tell what, why, and how. Some kinds of writing that explain are instructions, how-to paragraphs, and problem-solution paragraphs.

● To Narrate

To narrate means to tell a story with a beginning, middle, and end. Some examples of narrative writing include true stories, fiction stories, and biographies.

● To Persuade

To persuade means to convince someone else to do something or think a certain way. Some examples are persuasive and opinion essays and book reviews.

Understanding Task, Audience, and Purpose (TAP)

You should also think about your **audience**, or for whom you are writing. For example, the words you use in writing to a friend are likely to be different from those you use with someone you have never met.

You must also choose your **task**, or writing form. For example, if you want to tell your classmates about a topic you have been studying, you can share the information as a report, an essay, or a presentation.

Before you start to write, decide your task, audience, and purpose, or **TAP**. Your task is what you are writing. Your audience is for whom you are writing. Your purpose is why you are writing. Your teacher may give you the TAP for an assignment. Sometimes you will choose on your own.

Ask yourself these questions.

Task: <u>What</u> am I writing?

Do I want to write a letter, a report, or something else?

Audience: For <u>whom</u> am I writing?

Am I writing for a teacher, myself, or someone else?

Purpose: <u>Why</u> am I writing?

Am I writing to persuade someone, to give information, or for another reason?

The Writing Process

The writing process is a strategy that has five stages. It helps you think of ideas. It also helps you to plan your writing. Finally, it helps you to make your writing better. The best part about the writing process is that you can go back to any of the stages while you're writing.

The writing process helps you move back and forth between the different stages of your writing.

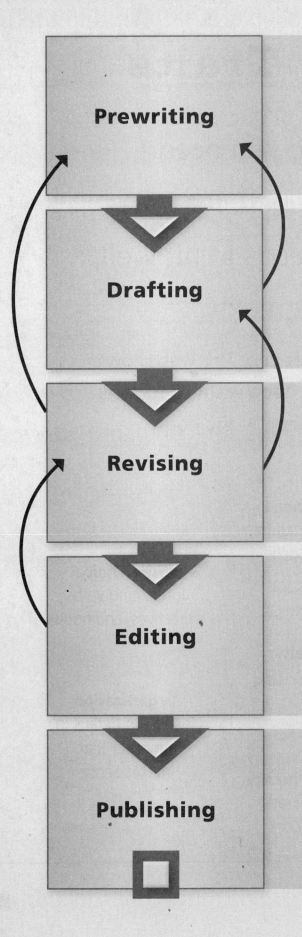

Prewriting

Think about your TAP—task, audience, and purpose. Then choose a topic. Gather and organize information about the topic.

Drafting

Put your ideas in writing. Don't worry about making mistakes. You can fix them later.

Revising

Read your writing to see if it matches your purpose. Meet with a partner to talk about how to make your draft better.

Editing

Fix your mistakes. Look for changes you should make in spelling, grammar, and capitalization.

Publishing

Decide how you want to publish your work. Share your writing with others.

The Writing Traits

To play a game well, you need special skills. In baseball, for example, a player needs to hit well, catch well, and run quickly.

Good writing takes special skills, too. This web shows the traits, or characteristics, of good writing. You will learn more about these traits later in the book.

Conventions
Correct punctuation, grammar, spelling

Ideas
Interesting, clear content supported by reasons and details

Word Choice
Interesting verbs, adjectives, and nouns

The Traits of Good Writing

Voice
Your own words and ideas

Organization
Ideas and details in an order that makes sense

Sentence Fluency
Different kinds of sentences

Traits Checklist

As you practice writing, ask yourself these questions.

☑ **Ideas**	Is my purpose clear? Do I stay on topic? Do I use details to support my ideas?
☑ **Organization**	Did I put my ideas in order? Do I have a beginning, middle, and ending? Do I use transitions to show time order?
☑ **Voice**	Do I write in my own words? Does my writing show who I am?
☑ **Word Choice**	Do I use specific nouns, strong verbs, and colorful adjectives?
☑ **Sentence Fluency**	Do my sentences go together? Are they easy to read?
☑ **Conventions**	Are my spelling, grammar, and punctuation correct?

Sentences That Tell a True Story

Sentences that tell a true story are always about events that have happened to a writer.

Parts of Sentences That Tell a True Story

- The words *I* and *me*
- Descriptive words that tell how the writer feels
- Events that really happened, told in time order
- Details that help the reader picture the story
- Transition words that show the order of events

Words *I* and *me*
Show that the writer was involved

Descriptive Words
Tell how the writer feels

Events
Tell what happened in time order

Details
Help the reader picture the story

I have a little black and white cat named Milo. He used to be afraid of his cat toys and the doorbell. **At first**, I thought it was cute. But **soon**, I felt sad for him. I wanted him to be brave and not to be afraid of everything. So I played gently with him so he could get used to cat toys. **Then** I rang the doorbell to show him it was not scary. **Now**, he is not afraid of anything except the vacuum cleaner. It is really loud!

Other Transitions
Next
During
After a while
Before
Later
Last

Name _____

Follow your teacher's directions to complete Frames 1 and 2.

1 One of the best days I ever had was when I _____

_____.

In the morning, I _____

_____. Later, _____

_____.

At the end of the day, I felt _____

_____.

2 _____

_____. In the beginning, _____

_____

_____. After that, _____

_____

_____. Finally, _____

_____.

3 On a separate sheet of paper, use your prewriting plan
to write sentences that tell a true story about your
favorite activity.

Friendly Letter

A **friendly letter** has five parts. You write a friendly letter to someone you know.

✏️ Parts of a Friendly Letter

- A heading, greeting, body, closing, and signature
- A reason for writing
- Interesting details
- Your thoughts and feelings

Heading
With date

Greeting
Who the letter is to, followed by a comma

Body
Interesting details in your own voice

Closing
Gets a comma

Signature
Your name

300 Knox Street

Maitland, FL 32751

October 3, 2012

Dear Luke,

   We had so much fun at the farm today. **First,** we went on a hayride. We sat on piles of soft hay.

   Next, we picked pumpkins. My pumpkin was so heavy. I had a hard time lifting it.

   Later on, we all drank fresh apple juice. I wish you had been there, too.

                 Your friend,
                 Sara

Other Closings
Sincerely
Regards
Best regards
Yours truly
Very truly yours
Love
Your pal

Follow your teacher's directions to complete this page.

1 _____

_____

_____

Dear _____

We had the best time at the water park. First, _____

_____

_____. Next, _____

_____

_____. Later on, _____

_____

_____.

_____

_____

2 On a separate sheet of paper, plan and write a short friendly letter to your teacher. Include all five parts.

3 On a separate sheet of paper, use your prewriting plan to write a friendly letter, or make a new plan to write a letter about a different event. Include all five parts.

Sentences That Describe

Sentences that describe tell the reader all about a person, place, thing, or feeling. They use our senses to show how things look, smell, taste, feel, and sound.

Parts of Sentences That Describe

- One main idea
- Sense words
- Details that are grouped in an order that makes sense

One Main Idea
Describes one thing at a time

Sense Words
Use sights, sounds, tastes, smells, and textures to describe

Details
Are grouped in a way that makes sense

Summer is my very favorite time of year. All of the leaves on the trees are green. The wind blows through them all day. The sun is warm and bright. The grass feels soft on my feet when I take off my shoes. I can smell the flowers and hear the bees buzzing in them. The flowers are pink and yellow and green. They grow near the sidewalk and in front of the porch. But I like summer the best because I can play outside!

Other Sense Words
Round
Blue
Sour
Fast
Loud
Fuzzy
Yellow
Dusty

Follow your teacher's directions to complete Frames 1 and 2.

We Do 1 When I look outside the window, I can see _____.

_____

The air outside feels _____

_____

_____. I can hear the sound of _____

_____

I can smell _____

_____

We Do 2 _____

_____. Its shape is _____

_____

_____. It feels _____

_____

_____. When it moves, it sounds _____

_____

You Do 3 On a separate sheet of paper, use your prewriting plan to describe your favorite activity, or make a new plan to write about a room you like to be in.

True Story: Prewriting

A **true story** is always about something real that happened.

Parts of a True Story

- One event that really happened
- A clear beginning, middle, and end
- A starting sentence that tells the main idea
- Important details told in time order

Brainstorming List

- First day of school
- How I found Lucky
- Our new backyard
- Painting the playroom

How I Found Lucky

Crying in the grass

↓

Could not walk or get up

↓

Grandma took her to the animal hospital

↓

The vet fixed her up

Name _____

Follow your teacher's directions to complete this page.

 1 **a. List of ideas**

_____   _____

_____   _____

_____   _____

b. Title or Topic: _____

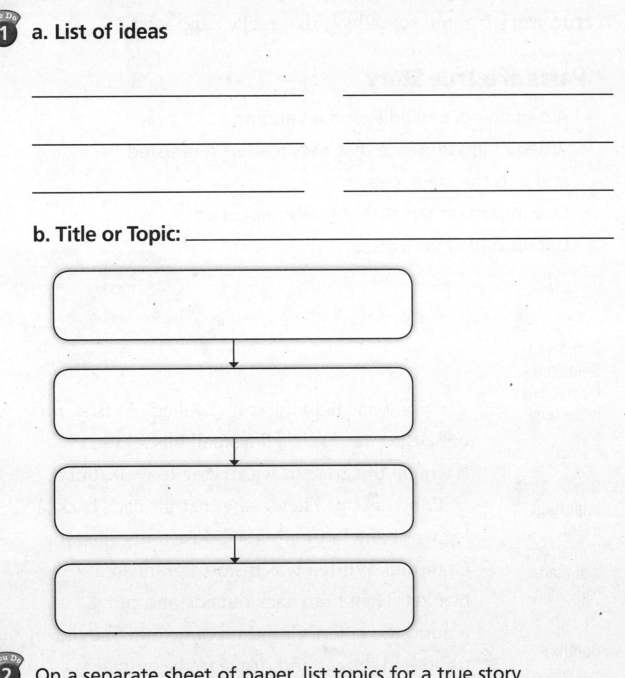

 2 On a separate sheet of paper, list topics for a true story you want to write. Choose a topic. Then fill in a flow chart with details about that topic.

3 On another sheet of paper, plan a true story, or use what you have learned to improve another plan.

True Story

A **true story** is about something that really happened.

✏️ Parts of a True Story

- A beginning, a middle, and an ending
- A beginning sentence that gets readers interested and tells the main idea
- One important event that really happened
- Details told in time order

Beginning Sentence
Begins in an interesting way

One Important Event
Something that really happened

Details
Tell what happened in time order

Ending
One or more sentences that wrap up the story

"Someone help the cat!" I yelled. **At first**, no one heard me. I noticed a small black kitten crying in the grass. It was trying to walk, but it couldn't get up. **Then** I saw that the cat's back leg was bent. I ran into the house and called for Grandma. **While** I was inside, I grabbed a blanket. Then I ran back outside and put it around the kitten. Grandma came out. She put us both in the car and drove to the animal hospital. The wonderful animal doctor was able to fix her up. **Later**, the cat was fine, and I was happy. I now had a kitten I named Lucky.

Other Transitions
First
Next
After that
During
Last
Finally

Name _____

Follow your teacher's directions to complete this page.

1 Boom! I heard a loud crash from our dining room.

At first, _____

_____. Then _____

_____

_____. While _____

_____.

_____. I was so _____

_____

Later, _____

_____. Next, _____

_____. After that, _____

_____. Finally, _____

_____

_____

2 On a sheet of paper, write a true story about a time you tried something new.

3 On a sheet of paper, use your prewriting plan to write a true story. If you like, make a new plan and write about something that happened to you.

Informational Paragraph

An **informational paragraph** gives facts about one main idea or topic. An informational paragraph also gives details that support the main idea.

Parts of an Informational Paragraph

- A topic sentence that states the main idea
- Supporting details that tell about the main idea
- Facts that can be proved true
- A closing statement that ties ideas together

Topic Sentence
Tells the topic and main idea

Supporting Details
Facts that tell more about the main idea

Polar bears live in dens in the far north. They dig the dens out of snow and ice. Their fur helps them stay warm in their cold, snowy homes. **Sometimes** they dig their homes in the middle of a snow bank. Most polar bears dig their dens in the fall. **Then** they give birth to cubs in the winter. The mother bear stays in the den with the cubs until the spring. She helps keep them safe. A polar bear's den makes a good home.

Other Transitions
First
Next
One thing
Another thing
Another example
Also
At times

Name _____

Follow your teacher's directions to complete Frames 1 and 2.

We Do 1   Many animals build nests, but beavers build _____.

_____

_____. (detail) _____

_____.

_____. (detail) _____

_____

(detail) _____

You Do 2   _____

_____. (detail) _____

_____

_____. (detail) _____

_____

_____. (detail) _____

_____

You Do 3   On a separate sheet of paper, use your prewriting plan to write an informational paragraph. If you like, make a new plan to write about a different animal home.

Informational Paragraph

An **informational paragraph** explains all about a person, a place, a thing, or even an activity.

Parts of an Informational Paragraph

- A topic sentence that starts the paragraph
- Facts and details that explain the main idea
- A closing sentence that ties ideas together

Topic Sentence
Introduces the main idea

Facts and Details
Explain the main idea to the reader

Closing Sentence
Finishes the paragraph

A big, brown groundhog lives in a hole in my backyard. I watch our groundhog come out in the afternoons to eat all of the vegetables in our garden. Groundhogs have bodies that help them live outside. **For example**, they have strong muscles for digging deep holes. They **also** have sharp teeth for eating tough weeds and plants. Groundhogs are afraid of people. They can run fast, **too**. When my mom yells at our groundhog for eating her garden, he quickly runs right back to his hole!

Other Words That Support the Main Idea
First
Then
Sometimes
Another
Lastly

Name _____

Follow your teacher's directions to complete Frames 1 and 2.

1 One animal that I know a lot about is a _____

_____ .

First, this animal has _____

_____

_____ . Also, _____

_____ . For example, _____

_____ .

The best thing about this animal is _____

_____ .

2 _____ .

_____ . Sometimes _____

_____

_____ . In addition, _____

_____ . Last, _____

_____ .

 On a separate sheet of paper, use your prewriting plan
to write about a favorite activity, or make a new plan
to write about an invention you would like to make.

Informational Paragraph

An **informational paragraph** explains something to a reader. It uses facts and definitions to explain and inform.

✏️ Parts of an Informational Paragraph

- A topic sentence that tells the main idea
- Supporting details that tell important facts about the main idea
- A closing sentence that finishes the paragraph

Topic Sentence
Begins the paragraph

Supporting Details
Tell important facts about the main idea

Closing Sentence
Finishes the paragraph

Rain water can be used for lots of things. Every time it rains, my mom puts out a big bucket. When it fills up with water, she puts the bucket on the porch. She uses the water for her plants inside the house. **Also**, she uses the water to rinse my mud projects off the sidewalk. Rain water is good for outside plants, **too**. When it gets hot and sunny, we use the bucket of water for the garden. Mom says we are conserving water. That **means** that we are saving it for a rainy day!

Other Words that Support the Main Idea
In addition
Plus
Next
For example
Last
Then

Name _____

Follow your teacher's directions to complete Frames 1 and 2.

1 Rainy days can be fun for _____

_____.

One thing to do is _____

_____. Rainy days are also good for _____

_____

_____. Sometimes _____

_____

In the end, _____

_____.

2 _____

_____. For example, _____

_____

_____. That means _____

_____. Finally, _____

_____.

3 On a separate sheet of paper, use your prewriting plan
to write an informative paragraph, or make a new
plan to write about a game or hobby.

Instructions: Prewriting

Instructions tell readers how to do something. They include all the steps in order from the beginning to the end.

Parts of Instructions

- A list of materials
- All of the steps in time order
- A clear beginning, middle, and end

Brainstorming List

- How to set the alarm clock
- How to tie a shoe
- How to make a peanut butter and jelly square
- How to plant flower seeds

Topic: Peanut Butter and Jelly Squares

You need two slices of bread, peanut butter, two kinds of jelly, a knife, a spoon, and a plate.

↓

Cut bread into squares. Spread peanut butter on squares.

↓

Spread on two kinds of jelly.

↓

Put jelly-side down on peanut butter squares.

Name _____

Follow your teacher's directions to complete this page.

How to Plant Flower Seeds

Materials:

Seeds   Flower Pot

Dirt and water   Spoon

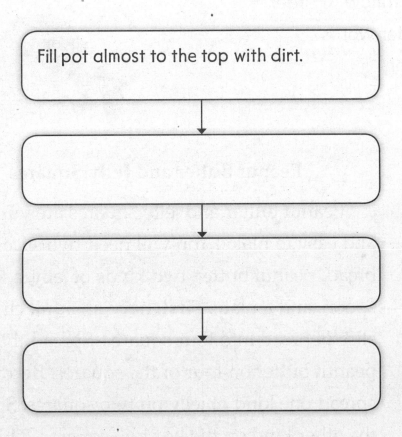

Fill pot almost to the top with dirt.

2 On a separate sheet of paper, list topics for instructions that you want to write. Choose a topic. Then fill in a flow chart with details about that topic.

3 On another sheet of paper, plan a set of instructions, or use what you have learned to improve another plan.

Instructions

Instructions tell how to do something. They give steps to follow. Instructions have time-order words to help you write the steps in order.

Parts of Instructions

- Materials your readers need
- Steps to follow in order
- Time-order words
- An ending

What You Need
Lists the things you will need

Steps
What you need to do in order

Time-Order Words
Tell you when to do each step

Ending
Why you should do this

Peanut Butter and Jelly Squares

Peanut butter and jelly squares are yummy and easy to make! You will need two slices of bread, peanut butter, two kinds of jelly, a knife, a spoon, and a plate. **First**, have an adult cut each slice of bread into four squares. Spread the peanut butter on four of the squares. **Second**, spread one kind of jelly on two squares. Spread the other kind on the last two squares. **Third**, place the jelly squares jelly side down onto the peanut butter squares. **Then** place them on a plate. Now you have four yummy squares to eat!

Other Transitions
Begin
Start
Next
Then
Last
Finally

Name _____

Follow your teacher's directions to complete the frame.

1 _____

You will need _____

_____

_____.

First, _____

_____

_____. Second, _____

_____

_____

Third, _____

_____. Fourth, _____

_____. Last, _____

_____

_____.

2 On a separate sheet of paper, write a set of instructions that explain how to make your favorite craft project.

3 On a separate sheet of paper, use your prewriting plan to write instructions, or make a new plan and write a different set of instructions.

Persuasive Letter

A **persuasive letter** is addressed to a single reader. It makes a request and gives reasons for the request.

Parts of a Persuasive Letter

- Heading, greeting, body, closing, and signature
- A goal, or request
- Detailed reasons for the request
- An ending that ties things together

Heading & Greeting
Tell the writer's address, when the letter was written, and to whom it was sent

249 N. Morris Street
Fort Myers, FL 33901
November 10, 2013

Mrs. Rosemary Harris
14 West Sutter Street
Fort Myers, FL 33901

Dear Mrs. Harris,

Body
States the goal, or request, and reasons for the request

Our class would like a longer recess. The fresh air outside is good for our bodies. Exercise helps us, too. It is easier to sit still in class after we have run and played. Longer recess

Ending
Ties ideas together

will help us learn and behave better.

Closing & Signature
Ends the letter

Thank you,
Your Students

Other Linking Words that Support Your Goal
In addition
Plus
Often
Because
Sometimes
Then

Name _____

Follow your teacher's directions to complete the frame.

_____

_____

_____

_____

_____

Dear _____,

    Our community needs to make changes to _____

_____.

One reason is because _____

Also, _____

Finally, _____

_____.

_____,

_____

 On a separate sheet of paper, write a persuasive letter to your school's principal. Be sure to state your goal and give reasons.

 On a separate sheet of paper, plan and write a persuasive letter to your community newspaper.

Opinion Paragraph

An **opinion paragraph** tells about an opinion, or the idea a writer has about something. It explains all of the reasons why the writer holds that opinion.

Parts of an Opinion Paragraph

- An opinion that uses clear words and shows how you feel about the topic
- Strong reasons that support and explain your opinion
- An ending that repeats your opinion, using different words

Opinion
Tells what the writer thinks about a topic

Strong Reasons
Explain why the writer feels that way

Ending
Repeats the opinion in different words

A ukulele is a great instrument for kids to learn to play. It is a lot like a guitar, **only** smaller. That means it is easier for a kid to hold. A guitar has six strings, **but** a ukulele only has four. It is easier to play **because** there are fewer strings. The ukulele comes in lots of different shapes and colors. You can even get a red ukulele or one with your favorite picture painted on it. The **best** reason for learning how to play a ukulele is that you can show off your singing talents. I think every kid should learn how to play a ukulele.

Other Linking Words that Connect Opinions and Reasons
In addition
Plus
Often
Finally
And

Name _____

Follow your teacher's directions to complete Frames 1 and 2.

1   The drums are the most difficult instrument to play because

_____ .

Another reason is because _____

_____ . But _____

_____ . Sometimes _____

_____

In my opinion, _____

_____ .

2   _____

_____ . Also, _____

_____

_____ . Another reason _____

_____ . And so, _____

_____

_____

 3 On a separate sheet of paper, use your prewriting plan
to write an opinion paragraph, or make a new plan to
write about why it is important to try new things.

Persuasive Paragraph

A **persuasive paragraph** gives your opinion. It tries to make your readers think or do something.

Parts of a Persuasive Paragraph

- A topic sentence that states your opinion
- Reasons why you feel that way
- Examples for the reasons
- An ending that tries to make your readers agree with you

Topic Sentence
States your opinion

Reasons
Why you feel that way

Examples
Details that support your opinion

Ending
Tries to get your readers to agree with you

    I think teachers should give homework on Fridays. We get homework every other night during the week. Why should Friday be different? **First**, I think that homework is fun. It helps me remember what we did in class. **Second**, it does not take that long to do. It would not take time away from playing on the weekend. **Also**, there is more time for my family to help me on the weekend. We should all ask to have homework over the weekend.

Other Transitions
Because
First of all
Next
Often
Then
Last
Finally

Name _____

Follow your teacher's directions to complete Frames 1 and 2.

1 I think that _____. First, _____

_____.

Second, _____

_____

_____

_____. Also, _____

_____

_____.

2 We think that _____

_____. First of all, _____

_____

_____. Next, _____

_____. _____

_____. Finally, _____

_____

3 On a separate sheet of paper, use your prewriting plan
to write a persuasive paragraph, or make a new plan
to write a persuasive paragraph about school.

Persuasive Essay: Prewriting

A **persuasive essay** tells about a goal and explains why the goal is important.

Parts of a Persuasive Essay

- A beginning that states a clear goal, or something you want readers to do
- Middle paragraphs that tell reasons why the goal is important
- Facts that explain more about each reason
- An ending that states the goal in a different way

Brainstorming List
- Putting seat belts on school buses
- Learning how to swim
- Having a safety buddy
- Eating fruits and vegetables

Can help you if you get lost

Can hold your hand

Topic
Having a Safety Buddy

Can call for help

Can help you to remember things

Name _____

Follow your teacher's directions to complete this page.

 1 **a.**

Putting seat belts in   Learning how to swim
    school buses

Eating fruits and vegetables   Eating a good breakfast

Raising money for the local fire department

b.

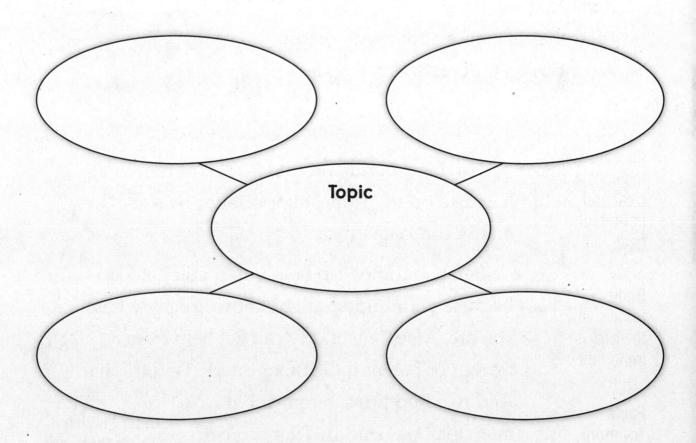

Topic

 2 On a separate sheet of paper, list topics for a
persuasive essay you want to write. Choose a topic.
Then fill in a flow chart with details about that topic.

 3 On another sheet of paper, plan a persuasive essay, or
use what you have learned to improve another plan.

Persuasive Essay

A **persuasive essay** names a clear goal and explains why the goal is important. It also shows ways the reader can reach that goal.

Parts of a Persuasive Essay

- An introduction that includes a clear goal
- A body that gives reasons why the goal is important
- Facts that tell more about each reason
- A conclusion that restates the goal

Introduction
Includes a clear and important goal

Having a buddy around is a lot of fun. But having a buddy is most important because a buddy can keep you safe.

Body
Shows why the goal is important

Safety buddies can help you if you get lost **because** your buddy might know exactly where you are. **Also**, one buddy can get help from a teacher or parent if the other buddy is in trouble. And two buddies can remember more than one buddy. That can help

Facts
Tell more about each reason

you to avoid trouble, **too**.

Conclusion
Repeats the goal using different words

Everyone should have a safety buddy with them at all times. It can help you stay safe and have fun!

Other Linking Words that Support Your Goal
In addition
Often
Finally
Then
For example

Name _____

Follow your teacher's directions to complete the frame.

1 Our school should _____

_____ .

The most important reason _____

_____

_____ . For example, _____

_____ .

It is good because _____

_____

_____ .

Then, kids can _____ .

_____

I think _____

_____ .

2 On a separate sheet of paper, write a persuasive essay to your school's principal. Include all of the parts of a persuasive essay.

3 On a separate sheet of paper, use your prewriting plan to write a persuasive essay, or plan and write a persuasive essay about exercising before going to bed at night.

Fictional Narrative Paragraph

A **fictional narrative paragraph** is a short story that a writer has made up. It has a clear beginning and ending.

Parts of a Fictional Narrative Paragraph

- A beginning sentence that introduces the characters and setting
- Details that tell more about the characters and setting
- Action that tells what is happening

Beginning Sentence
Introduces the characters and setting

Details
Tell about the characters and setting

Action
Puts events in time order

Mark's favorite thing to do in his playroom is to dress up. Today, Mark has decided to dress up as his Daddy, who is Mark's favorite person. First, Mark picks out the **biggest** shirt that he can find in Daddy's closet. Then, he puts on a **warm**, **blue** sweater that comes down to his knees. Wearing Daddy's clothes makes Mark feel **silly** and **happy** at the same time. But his costume isn't finished yet. Finally, he puts on Daddy's **orange** and **purple** tie. Perfect!

Kinds of Details
Colors
Shapes
Sizes
Sounds
Feelings
Actions

Follow your teacher's directions to complete Frames 1 and 2.

We Do 1 We had a great time at my dog's surprise party. First, we saw

_____ .

In the next room, we heard _____

_____ . We played _____

_____ . Then we all ate _____

_____ .

The best part of the party was _____

_____ .

You Do 2 _____

_____ . Next, _____

_____ . We saw _____

_____ . Finally, _____

_____

_____

_____ .

You Do 3 On a separate sheet of paper, use your prewriting plan
to write a fictional narrative paragraph, or make a
new plan to write about a holiday parade.

Fictional Narrative Paragraph

A **fictional narrative paragraph** is a short story that has a clear beginning and end. It can seem like a true story, but it is a made up story.

Parts of a Fictional Narrative Paragraph

- Details that describe the characters, setting, and events
- Dialogue that shows what characters are like and the exact words they say
- Events told in an order that makes sense

Details
Help the reader imagine the story

Dialogue
Shows what the characters are like

Events
Told in time order

"Try my new recipe," my mom said. She put a bowl of greenish-yellow soup in front of me.

"**Aw**, do I have to?" I asked.

Mom loves to cook. But she isn't very good at it. "Yes, you have to," Mom said firmly. "You'll like it, **sweetie**."

I looked at the soup. There were corn and carrots in it. At last, I took one tiny, super-small taste.

"Mom! It's **awesome**!" Finally, Mom had made something I liked!

Words that describe dialogue
I asked
She said
He explained
I cried
We shouted

Name _____

Follow your teacher's directions to complete Frames 1 and 2.

1 It was my first time _____.

My teacher began, saying, " _____

_____."

It was hard. I told her, " _____

_____."

Finally, _____

_____

_____. My teacher smiled and said," _____

_____."

2 _____

_____

_____. Next, _____

_____

_____. In the end, _____

_____.

We all said, " _____."

3 On a separate sheet of paper, use your prewriting plan to write a fictional narrative paragraph, or make a new plan to write about trying something new for the first time.

Descriptive Paragraph

A **descriptive paragraph** uses sense words to tell about a person, place, or thing.

Parts of a Descriptive Paragraph

- A topic sentence that tells what is being described
- Details that tell what you see, hear, feel, smell, and sometimes taste
- Words that describe color, shape, and size

Topic Sentence
Tells what is being described

Details
Help you picture what is described

Words
Tell about color, shape, and size

One of my favorite places is the park. The park's **giant** trees are filled with hundreds of **little chirping** birds on the branches. The park also has a **soft green** lawn to play on. The grass **smells sweet** after it is first cut. My brother and I often play catch there. The new playground nearby has a **long yellow** slide. I have to climb a **tall** ladder to get to the top. The park is a great place to play!

Some Color, Shape, and Size Words
red
round
square
huge
small
tiny

Name _____

Follow your teacher's directions to complete Frames 1 and 2.

We Do
1   A fun place is _____.

(see) _____

(hear) _____

(smell) _____

_____. (feel)

_____

_____. That is why the _____

_____ is a fun place!

You Do
2   _____

_____. (see) _____.

_____

_____. (hear) _____.

_____

(smell) _____.

(feel) _____.

You Do
3 On a sheet of paper, use your prewriting plan to write
a descriptive paragraph. If you like, make a new plan
to write about a place near your home.

Fictional Story: Prewriting

A **fictional story** is made up. It has characters, a plot, and a setting.

Parts of a Fictional Story

- A beginning, middle, and ending
- A plot with a problem that gets solved
- Action told in time order
- Dialogue, or words spoken by the characters

Brainstorming List

- (Mrs. Lee's bird comes to visit)
- Chef Primo burns the dinner
- A day at the zoo
- Taking care of Simba the cat

Title: When Mrs. Lee's Bird Came to Visit

Setting	Characters
the living room	Max and Molly
outside	Mom
	Mrs. Lee and her bird

Plot
Beginning
Max and Molly hear someone outside yelling for a cookie.
Middle
It is a bird that is yelling. The bird belongs to Mrs. Lee.
End
Max and Molly return the bird.

Name _____

Follow your teacher's directions to complete this page.

Setting	Characters
A spooky cabin in the woods	Jacob and his dog

Plot

Beginning

Jacob's dog starts barking loudly at the front door.

Middle

End

2 Choose one group of characters for a fictional story. Then, on a separate piece of paper, fill in a story map to plan your story.

A stray dog and cat   Three ladybugs

A dad and his two children   Two best friends

Two brothers   Lightning and thunder

3 On another sheet of paper, plan a fictional story, or use what you have learned to improve another plan.

Fictional Story

A **fictional story** is made up and tells what happens to one or more characters. It also has a setting and a plot.

Parts of a Fictional Story

- A beginning, a middle, and an ending
- A plot with a problem that gets solved
- Events told in time order
- Dialogue, or words spoken by the characters, in quotation marks

Dialogue
Tells exactly what characters say

Beginning
Has a problem to be solved

Middle
Events told in order

Ending
Tells how the problem was solved

"Cookie! Cookie! I want Cookie."

Max and Molly jumped. **All at once**, Max looked at Molly and said, "Who said that?" The voice came from the flower box outside.

Seconds later, Max and Molly ran to the window. Sitting in the daisies was a yellow bird.

Molly said, "Mom, look. That bird keeps saying it wants a cookie."

Mom laughed. "I think that's Mrs. Lee's bird. Mrs. Cookie Lee. She lives across the street."

Molly and Max **soon** returned the bird. Mrs. Lee was so happy!

Other Transitions
After
After that
At first
During
Meanwhile
Last
At last
Finally
Then

Name _____

Follow your teacher's directions to complete the frame.

1 "I want to go to the zoo today," said Lucy. _____

_____. All at once, _____

_____.

Seconds later, _____

_____.

_____.

" _____," said _____

_____. At first, _____

_____.

_____.

_____. Then _____

_____.

_____. At last, _____

_____.

2 On a sheet of paper, write a fictional story about a new pet.

3 On a sheet of paper, use your prewriting plan to write a fictional story. If you like, make a new plan to write a story about a hero.

Problem-Solution Paragraph

A **problem-solution paragraph** describes a problem.
Then it tells how to fix the problem.

Parts of a Problem-Solution Paragraph

- A problem that needs to be fixed
- Details that explain the whole problem
- A way to solve the problem

Problem
Tells what needs to be fixed

Details
Explain all the parts of the problem

Solution
Gives a clear way to fix the problem

The problem at our house is that the squirrels keep eating the bird seed we put out for the birds. Every day, Dad fills up the bird feeder. Later in the day, we see a **big**, **gray** squirrel sitting in the feeder. He **quickly** stuffs all the seeds he can into his mouth. Sometimes, he eats every seed in the feeder. He also scares off the **hungry** birds, so they do not get any seeds. Dad had a good idea, though. We put a **big** plate of seeds on the ground under the bird feeder. The squirrel eats what is on the plate. The birds use the feeder. Everyone is **happy**.

Words That Show Details
Huge
Fast
Fuzzy
Glassy
Loud
Purple
Sweet
Smelly

Name _____

Follow your teacher's directions to complete Frames 1 and 2.

1 A messy bedroom is a problem because _____

_____. It is a big problem when _____

_____

One quick way to fix the problem is _____

_____.

That way, _____

_____.

2 _____

_____. First, it is

a huge problem when _____

_____.

It is easy to solve this by _____

_____

_____.

3 On a separate sheet of paper, use your prewriting plan
to write a problem-solution paragraph, or make a new
plan to write about a problem you have choosing just
the right gift for a friend.

Compare-Contrast Paragraph

A **compare-contrast paragraph** tells how things are different and how they are alike. The subjects can be people, animals, places, or things.

Parts of a Compare-Contrast Paragraph

- A topic sentence that states the main idea
- Sentences that tell how things are different and how they are similar
- Details that help tell differences and similarities
- An ending that ties ideas together

Topic Sentence
States the main idea

Transition Words
Help connect ideas

Details
Show how the subjects are alike or different

Ending
Ties ideas together

    My sister and I are very **different**. People are surprised that we come from the same family. **First of all,** I love the color purple. My sister likes blue best. **Second**, I play music, **but** my sister paints pictures. **Third**, I love to wear dresses, **but** my sister will only wear jeans. However, we are alike in some ways. My sister and I can run fast. We play soccer together. Although we are different in many ways, we still love each other very much!

Other Transitions
Even though
Another difference
Unlike
On the other hand

Name _____

Follow your teacher's directions to complete the frame.

1 _____ and _____ are very alike. _____

First of all, _____.

Second, _____

_____

_____. Third, _____

_____.

On the other hand, they are different, too. _____

_____

_____

_____

_____

_____.

2 On a separate sheet of paper, write a paragraph that compares and contrasts two people you know.

3 Use your prewriting plan to write a compare-contrast paragraph, or make a new plan to write a paragraph that compares and contrasts two games.

Informational Paragraph

An **informational paragraph** tells facts and details about a person, place, or thing.

Parts of an Informational Paragraph

- An interesting topic sentence that tells the main idea
- Details that support and explain the main topic
- Facts that are told in an order that makes sense

Topic Sentence
Tells the main idea, or topic

Details
Support and explain the main idea

Order
Presents facts and details in a way that makes sense

Making a play toy for a cat is very easy. First, cut a **rectangle** out of a piece of cloth. Fold the rectangle in half to make a **square**. Next, use fabric glue along two edges. Leave the third edge open. When the glue dries, stuff catnip inside the square until it is **full** and **round**. Catnip is a plant that cats just **love**. Glue the last edge to shut the square. Finally, when it is all dry, give it to your cat. You will have a **happy** cat to play with!

Details that Help With Word Choice
Sounds
Shapes
Textures
Sights
Smells

Name _____

Follow your teacher's directions to complete Frames 1 and 2.

We Do
1   It is easy to pack a bag for a vacation or sleepover. First, _____

_____. Then, get

out _____.

After that, pack _____

_____

_____. Always remember to _____

_____.

Finally, _____

_____.

You Do
2   _____

_____. When this happens, _____.

Then, _____.

Finally, _____

_____

_____.

You Do
3 On a separate sheet of paper, use your prewriting plan
to write an informational paragraph, or make a new
plan to write about a craft project.

Research Report: Prewriting

A **research report** tells facts and information about a topic. It has an introduction, a body, and a conclusion.

Parts of a Research Report

- An interesting introduction, or topic sentence, that names the main idea
- A body with facts and details about the topic
- Illustrations, when helpful
- A conclusion that wraps up the report

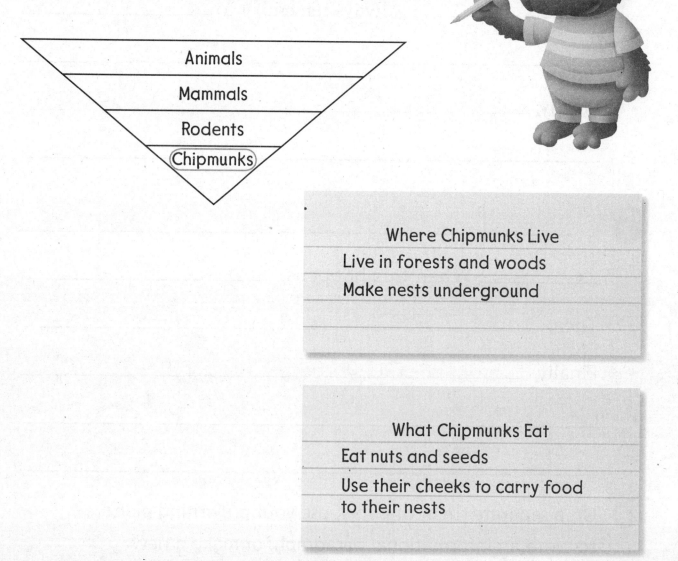

Animals

Mammals

Rodents

Chipmunks

Where Chipmunks Live
Live in forests and woods
Make nests underground

What Chipmunks Eat
Eat nuts and seeds
Use their cheeks to carry food to their nests

Name _____

Follow your teacher's directions to complete this page.

 1 **a.**

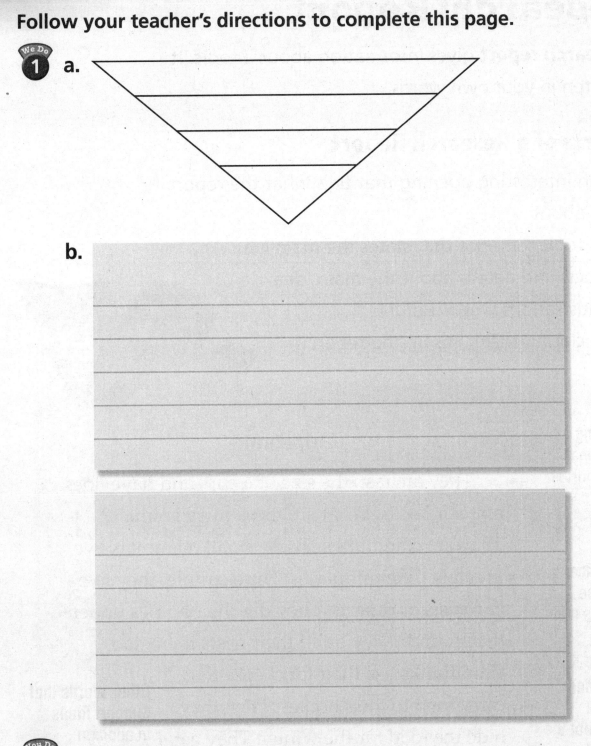

b.

2 On a separate sheet of paper, list topics for a research report. Choose one topic. Then write details about the topic on note cards.

3 On another sheet of paper, plan a research report, or use what you have learned to improve another plan.

Research Report

A **research report** gives information about a topic. It is written in your own words.

Parts of a Research Report

- An interesting opening that tells what the report is about
- A topic sentence that states the main idea
- Facts and details about the main idea
- Illustrations when useful
- A closing that sums up the report

Opening
Tells what the report is about

Topic Sentence
Tells the report's main idea

Facts and Details
Tell about the main idea

Closing
Sums up the report

Chipmunks

They are fast, the size of a cup, and have lines on their backs. What are these furry animals? They are chipmunks! These small mammals live in many different places. **For example**, they live in forests or deserts. They dig their homes under the ground. They build their nests there, too. Chipmunks use their fat cheeks to carry food to their homes. Then they hide the food for the winter. They eat foods **like** bugs, nuts, mushrooms, and seeds. Chipmunks are busy little animals!

Other Words that Support Ideas
In addition
Another
First
Second
Last
Finally
To sum up

Follow your teacher's directions to complete the frame.

We Do
1 Did you know that groundhogs are a kind of squirrel?

_____

_____

_____

_____. For example, _____

_____. In addition, _____

_____

_____

_____. Another example is _____

_____

_____

_____.

You Do
2 On a separate sheet of paper, write a research report about a stegosaurus, or any other dinosaur.

You Do
3 On a separate sheet of paper, use your prewriting plan to write a research report. If you like, make a new plan to write a research report about a different animal.

Response Poem

A **response poem** can be about a story. It can also be about the way that a story made you think or feel.

✏ Parts of a Response Poem

- Lines that may or may not rhyme
- Sensory words that describe the way things look, sound, taste, smell, or feel
- A musical beat, or rhythm

Rhyming Words
End each line with a similar sound

Sensory Words
Help readers picture the details

Rhythm
Can give each line a musical beat

On "The Mysterious Tadpole"

→ Louis has a funny **pet**

That has not finished growing **yet**.

He outgrows jars and sinks and **tubs**

And pools at all the swimming **clubs**.

→ Alphonse is green and huge, but **sweet**.

He eats hamburgers as a **treat**.

And when Alphonse is at his **best**

→ He finds a sunken treasure **chest**.

Alphonse can play, and he can **swim**.

I wish I had a pet like **him**.

Rhyming Words
Treat / street
Great / skate
Hook / shook
Brown / gown
Rug / tug
Light / sight

Name _____

Follow your teacher's directions to complete Frames 1 and 2.

1 My Favorite Character: _____

_____ kind.

_____ mind.

_____ wear.

_____ hair.

_____ goes.

_____ shows.

2 _____

_____ bright.

_____.

_____ see.

_____.

_____ stay.

_____.

 3 On a separate sheet of paper, use your prewriting plan
to write a response poem, or make a new plan to
write a response poem about your favorite book.

Opinion Paragraph

An **opinion paragraph** states an opinion, or the way a writer feels about something. It then supports the opinion with facts and details.

Parts of an Opinion Paragraph

- A topic sentence that clearly states an opinion
- Facts, examples, and reasons that support the opinion
- Details that make the opinion clearer to the reader
- Linking words that organize the paragraph and connect ideas
- Ending sentence that repeats the opinion in different words

Topic Sentence
States the writer's opinion

Facts, Examples, and Reasons
Support the writer's opinion

Details
Describe the opinion

The playground near the public library is in bad shape. A few of the climbing structures are breaking. The red plastic is peeling off the stairs, **and** that makes them slippery. Even the old gate is broken. That means little kids can leave the playground when their parents are not watching. It was a fun park to play in, **but** now no one goes there because it is too old. We need to ask adults to rebuild the playground.

Other Linking Words that Organize
So that
Then
Also
In addition
Besides

Name _____

Follow your teacher's directions to complete the frame.

1 I am a good friend because _____

_____ .

In addition, I _____

_____

_____ . Also _____

_____ . Because

I am a good friend, _____

_____ .

Then, _____

_____ .

Besides, _____

_____

_____ . Most importantly, _____

_____ .

2 On a separate sheet of paper, write an opinion
paragraph about your favorite sport.

3 On a separate sheet of paper, use your prewriting plan to
write an opinion paragraph, or make a new plan to write
about a change you would like to see in your neighborhood.

Story Response Paragraph

A **story response paragraph** tells what the writer thinks and feels about a story. The details in the paragraph support the writer's opinion.

✏️ Parts of a Story Response Paragraph

- A topic sentence that clearly states an opinion
- Details and examples from the story that support the opinion
- Linking words that organize the paragraph and connect ideas
- A clear ending that states the writer's topic in a different way

Topic Sentence
States the writer's opinion

Details and Examples
Support the writer's opinion

Linking Words
Connect ideas and organize the paragraph

Clear Ending
States the writer's opinion again

The dog in The Dog That Dug for Dinosaurs by Shirley Raye Redmond is a very smart animal. **For example**, the dog helps to find dinosaur bones. Tray sniffs and scratches the ground to show where the bones are. **Also**, Tray knows how to guard the bones. He growls to keep people away from them. **Sometimes**, Tray seems to answer his owner's questions by wagging his tail. In the story, Mr. Buckland calls Tray an intelligent dog. That means he really is a very smart dog.

Other Words that Link Ideas
Besides
In addition
Next
Finally
Because

Name _____

Follow your teacher's directions to complete Frames 1 and 2.

 1 Story Title: _____

I thought this was a good story because _____

_____. In addition,

_____.

For example, _____

_____. Also, _____

_____.

Because of these reasons, _____

_____.

2 _____

_____

because _____

_____. Besides, _____

_____

_____. Finally, _____

_____.

3 On a separate sheet of paper, use your prewriting plan
to write a story response paragraph, or make a new
plan to write about a character from a story you like.

Response Essay: Prewriting

A **response essay** tells about a book you have read. It describes your feelings and thoughts about the book.

Parts of a Response Essay

- A first sentence that tells the title of the reading and your opinion of it
- Information about what you have read
- Details and reasons that support your opinion
- A closing sentence that sums up your opinion

Brainstorming List
- Now & Ben
- Two of Everything
- The Dog That Dug for Dinosaurs
- The Mysterious Tadpole

Title: Now & Ben Is Awesome

Reason #1: Ben Franklin invented some great things.	Reason #2: Ben Franklin changed our world.
Funny chairs A clock with a second hand The lightning rod	Electricity Libraries and hospitals Post offices Fire departments

Name _____

Follow your teacher's directions to complete this page.

1 **a. Three Books I Have Read**

_____

_____

_____

b. Title: _____

Reason #1: _____ _____	Reason #2: _____ _____

2 On a separate sheet of paper, choose another book as the topic of a response essay. Then fill in a Column Chart with reasons and details that support your opinion.

3 On another sheet of paper, plan a response essay, or use what you have learned to improve another plan.

Response Essay

A **response essay** tells about a selection you have read. It also tells your thoughts and feelings.

✏️ Parts of a Response Essay

- An opening that gives the selection's title and your opinion
- Information about what you read
- Reasons and details to support your opinion
- Linking words that connect opinions to reasons
- A closing to sum up your opinion

Opening
States title and your opinion

Reasons
Details that tell about the book and your opinion

Closing
Restates your opinion

    I think *Now & Ben* is a very good book. I learned that Ben Franklin invented many things. Some of his **best** inventions were funny chairs and a clock with a second hand. He helped us use electricity, and he invented the lightning rod.

    We should thank Ben for our libraries and hospitals, too. He also started post offices and fire departments. **I feel** everyone should read *Now & Ben* because Ben Franklin changed our world.

Opinion Words
I think
I feel
I like
I believe
Good
Wonderful
Best
Worst

Name _____

Follow your teacher's directions to complete the frame.

We Do 1 I think _____

_____ .

_____

_____ best _____

_____

_____

_____ . I feel _____

_____ .

I like _____

_____

_____

_____

_____ . I believe _____

_____ .

You Do 2 On a separate sheet of paper, write a response essay to a story you read in class this month.

You Do 3 On a separate sheet of paper, use your prewriting plan to write a response essay. If you like, make a new plan to write a response essay to a different story.

Prewriting

The **writing process** is a strategy that can help you write. It has five stages: prewriting, drafting, revising, editing, and publishing. **Prewriting** is the first stage.

Prewriting

- Prewriting means planning before you write. Plan by brainstorming ideas to write about.
- Some ways to brainstorm include making lists, clustering, using what you already know, or looking through your journal.
- After you brainstorm, choose one idea to write about. Circle it.
- Gather information on your chosen idea, or topic.

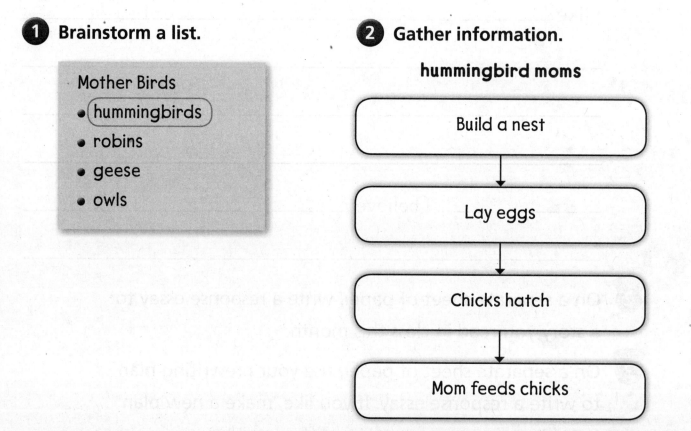

1 Brainstorm a list.

Mother Birds
- (hummingbirds)
- robins
- geese
- owls

2 Gather information.

hummingbird moms

Build a nest

↓

Lay eggs

↓

Chicks hatch

↓

Mom feeds chicks

3 **Organize the information.** Choose the Graphic Organizer that works best with your **TAP**. Here are some examples:

Cluster Chart for Informational Writing

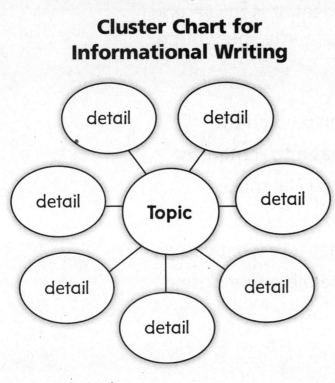

Venn Diagram to Compare and Contrast

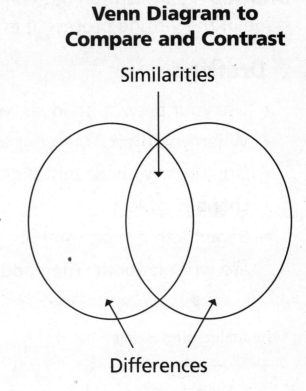

Idea-Support Map

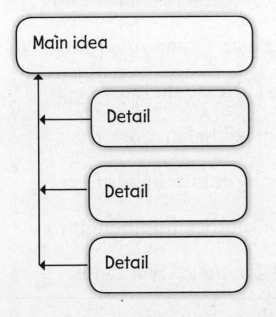

5 Ws Chart for Narratives

5 Ws Chart
Who?
What?
When?
Where?
Why?

Drafting

Drafting means writing out your ideas. It is the second stage in the writing process. It is done after prewriting.

✏ Drafting

- Use your prewriting ideas to help you draft.
- When you draft, turn your ideas into sentences.
- Don't worry about mistakes. You can make changes later.
- Begin with a topic sentence that tells what you are writing about. Then add details and a closing.

hummingbird moms

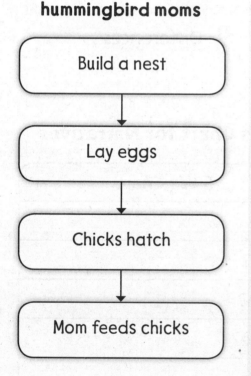

Draft

Hummingbird mothers do a lot to help bring their babies into the world. First, a hummingbird builds a nest. Next, she lays eggs. Soon, the chicks hatch from the eggs. The baby hummingbirds are hungry! The mother hummingbird brings food for them. She helps them until they grow up.

Another Example

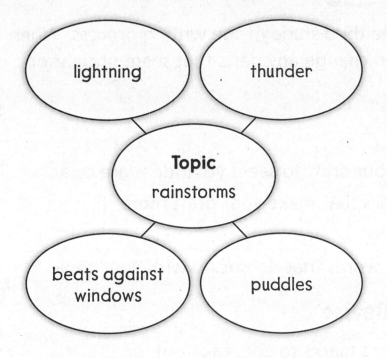

Draft

Rainstorms can be very exciting. Lightning makes huge flashes in the sky. Scary thunder can make you hide under the bed. Sometimes the rain beats hard against my windows and even makes them shake. The next day there are lots of puddles. If you want to see the sky put on a big show, you will like watching a rainstorm!

Revising

Revising is the third stage of the writing process. When you revise, you change any parts that seem unclear or incomplete.

Revising

- Reread your draft to see if your ideas are clear.
- Add details that make your draft more interesting.
- Take out words that do not go with your topic.

Ways to Revise

- Use editor's marks to add, take out, or change words in your draft.
- Add sentences to show more detail.

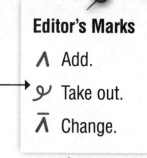

Editor's Marks

∧ Add.

℘ Take out.

λ̄ Change.

> First, a hummingbird builds a nest. She uses small sticks
> ∧
> and dandelion fuzz.

- Combine sentences to cut words you don't need.

> The mother builds a small nest. She builds it out of
> small sticks and dandelion fuzz.

two white

Next, she lays ∧eggs. Soon, the chicks hatch from the eggs.

- Move information so that it is in an order that makes sense.

∧The mother hummingbird brings food for them.

(The babies are hungry!)

Here's how a revised draft might look:

Hummingbird mothers do a lot to help bring

their babies into the world. First, a hummingbird
out of small sticks and dandelion fuzz.
two white
builds a nest∧ Next, she lays ∧eggs. Soon, the chicks

hatch from the eggs.∧The mother hummingbird brings

food for them. (The baby hummingbirds are hungry!)

She helps them until they grow up.

Editing

Editing is the fourth stage of the writing process. When you edit, you proofread your draft for mistakes. Then you correct any that you find.

Editing

- Proofread your draft and look for mistakes.
- Use editing marks to help you fix your writing.
- Check for complete sentences.
- Check for capital letters.
- Check for commas and end punctuation.
- Check for spelling and grammar errors.
- Use verbs and adjectives correctly.

Editor's Marks

∧ Add.

ℐ Take out.

⊼ Change.

Edited Draft

The mother builds a small nest out of tiny sticks and spider

webs⊙ She fills the nest with ~~dandylion~~ *dandelion* fluff and cattail fuzz.

cozy
The nest is warm and ~~cosy~~. Then she lays two white eggs.

The
~~the~~ eggs are the size of peas.

Publishing

Publishing means sharing your writing. It is the last stage of the writing process. In this stage, you make a clean, final draft of your writing.

✏ Publishing

- Write or type your final draft neatly, with margins and paragraph indents.
- Put your name on your work.
- Think of ways to share your writing, such as making it into a book, reading it aloud, or adding pictures.
- You can use a computer to choose pictures, charts, audio, or video to go with your writing.

Hummingbird Mothers
by Alice Montgomery

Hummingbird mothers do a lot to help bring their babies into the world. First, a hummingbird builds a nest out of small sticks and dandelion fuzz. Next, she lays two white eggs. Soon, the chicks hatch from the eggs. The baby hummingbirds are hungry! The mother hummingbird brings food for them. She helps them until they grow up.

Ideas

There are six traits to follow for good writing. The traits are ideas, organization, voice, word choice, sentence fluency, and conventions. **Ideas** are what you write about.

Ideas

- Can come from what you know or what you learn
- Are supported by interesting details
- Can come from brainstorming or making lists

Make a List of Topics

Think of as many ideas as you can and make a list. Circle the ideas you like the most.

People	Places	Things
(friends)	home	books
family	school	swing set
mom	library	skateboard
teacher	Florida	school bus
doctor	(science museum)	board game

Sample Writing Idea: Friends

The word <u>friends</u> makes me think of Jodi and Lisa. I could write a story about the time we took a field trip to the science museum.

Narrative Writing

Write down ideas about people and events.

Good graphic organizers to use for ideas: story map, flow chart

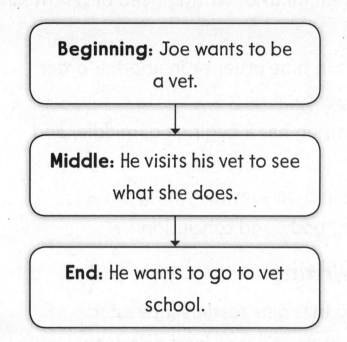

Beginning: Joe wants to be a vet.

Middle: He visits his vet to see what she does.

End: He wants to go to vet school.

Informative Writing

Make a list of details and questions about a topic.

Good graphic organizers to use for ideas: web, idea-support map

Ideas for a Report About Pandas

What kind of animal are pandas?

Where do pandas live?

How do pandas raise their young?

What do pandas eat?

Organization

Organization is the order in which you put your words and ideas. Different kinds of writing need different kinds of organization.

- Ideas can be in time order or in another order that makes sense.
- Narrative writing has a beginning, middle, and end.
- Informative and persuasive writing has an introduction, body, and conclusion.

Narrative Writing

- A beginning that gets readers interested
- A middle that describes at least one event
- An ending that tells how the event wrapped up

Beginning →   Jodi's mom took us to the zoo. Jodi did not want to go. She was afraid of ostriches. She said they were tall and ugly. Maybe one would bite her. I thought ostriches were weird-looking but cool. I really wanted to see one. We went to a

Middle → bird exhibit and saw an ostrich behind a fence. He seemed very friendly. He had a long neck and long legs and a big body with lots of feathers. The ostrich looked at us and ran away. Jodi

End → laughed. She is not afraid of ostriches anymore.

Information Writing

- An introduction that states the main idea
- A body with supporting details that tell about the main idea
- A closing statement that ties ideas together

Introduction →   Ostriches are unusual birds. For one thing, they can't fly. Instead, they can run very fast. Their long legs help them run up to 40 miles per **Body** → hour. They are also the biggest kind of bird in the world. They lay huge eggs, too. They look strange, with long necks and small heads. **Conclusion** → Ostriches are different from most birds.

Persuasive Writing

- A topic sentence that states your opinion
- Reasons and examples of why you feel that way
- An ending that tries to make your readers agree with you

Opinion →   Ostriches are the best kinds of birds. First, they are big! Second, they can run really fast. They have special claws on their feet that look like hooves. Those help move their feet. It is **Reasons** → okay that they can't fly because they can still move quickly. They also can hear and see very well. Ostriches are different from other kinds of **Ending** → birds. That makes them more interesting.

Voice

Voice shows what a writer is like.

✏ Voice

- You have your own style and voice.
- Use your voice to speak to your readers.
- Share how you think and feel.
- Whenever you write, keep your purpose in mind.
- Match your voice with your purpose. Are you writing to describe, tell a story, explain, or persuade?

Informative Voice

Use specific details to explain your topic. Help your reader to understand information or follow steps.

> First, spread glue on your drawing in the spots where you want the glitter to go. Next, sprinkle the glitter on the glue. Let it dry for a minute. Then shake the extra glitter off. Finally, let your picture dry.

Persuasive Voice

Use good reasons so that the reader will agree with you.

> It is always good to wear a hat on a cold day. You lose a lot of heat from the top of your head. A hat helps to keep your whole body warm.

Word Choice

The words you choose help create a picture for your reader.

Word Choice

- Choose words that best tell your ideas.
- Revise your work to change dull, unclear words. Replace them with exact words.

Exact Words

- Clearly describe what characters are thinking and feeling
- Clearly describe what is happening
- Make people, places, and things easy for readers to see

Not Exact

Lina went to Jake's party. She was happy to go. She had a gift. She hoped Jake liked it.

Exact

Lina skipped down the street on the way to Jake's birthday party. She was so excited to go. She brought a gift wrapped in colorful paper. She was sure Jake would like it, since he had been talking about it for weeks!

Sentence Fluency

Sentence fluency means a writer's sentences flow together smoothly. Sentence fluency makes your writing clearer and easier to read.

Sentence Fluency

- Make some sentences short or long.
- Connect ideas from sentence to sentence.
- Use different sentence beginnings.

Make some sentences short or long.

Sentences all the same length	Combine into longer, smoother ones
I like to ride my bike. I like to ride it downhill. It is fast.	I like to ride my bike. It is fun to ride it downhill fast.
The house was old. It was made of stone. It was made of wood, too.	The old house was made of stone and wood.

Connect ideas from sentence to sentence.

Choppy sentences	Use time-order words
I saw the rabbit in the garden. I saw the rabbit in the garden today.	Yesterday, I saw the rabbit in the garden. I saw him again today.

Use different sentence beginnings.

Too many sentences with the same beginning

Florida is the best state. Florida is not like other states. Florida is warm and sunny. It is near the ocean. You can enjoy the beach.

Variety of sentence beginnings

Florida is the best state. Unlike other states, it is warm and sunny. Since Florida is near the ocean, you can enjoy the beach.

Here is an example of how to fix sentences to make them more fluent in a paragraph.

Choppy First Draft

Birds live in different kinds of nests. Birds lay eggs in the nests. Birds take care of their babies in the nests. Nests come in many sizes and shapes. Nests are made from leaves or twigs.

Revised Draft

Birds live in different kinds of nests. They build their nests in many sizes and shapes. Most make their nests from twigs or leaves. The nests may look different, but all birds lay eggs in their nests and take care of their babies there, too.

Conventions

Conventions are rules for grammar, spelling, punctuation, and capitalization. When you edit your writing, you check for conventions.

 Conventions

- Follow grammar and punctuation rules.
- Check your spelling.
- Check your capitalization.
- Edit and proofread your writing.

Editing Checklist

Use an editing checklist to review your writing.

_____	My sentences are different lengths.
_____	My sentences are complete.
_____	I have used punctuation correctly.
_____	My words are all spelled correctly.
_____	I have used capitalization correctly.

Subjects and Predicates

A sentence should have both a subject and a predicate.

Wrong Way	Right Way
The roller coaster. Better than other rides.	The roller coaster is my favorite ride. I like it better than other rides.

Singular and Plural Nouns

Singular nouns are used for one person or thing. Plural nouns are used for more than one person or thing.

Wrong Way	Right Way
He wanted to make many friend. I put one ice cubes in my juice.	He wanted to make many friends. I put one ice cube in my juice.

Capitalization

Proper nouns should always be capitalized.

Wrong Way	Right Way
Next week, I am going to orlando with my brother ricardo.	Next week, I am going to Orlando with my brother Ricardo.

Correct use of commas in dates and places

Commas separate months and days from years. They are also used to separate cities or towns from states.

Wrong Way	Right Way
He was born on March, 31 2000 in Miami Florida.	He was born on March 31, 2000 in Miami, Florida.

Writing Workshop

In a writing workshop, you share your writing with others. You can help each other make your writing better.

✏ Being Part of a Writing Workshop

- Listen carefully to your classmates' ideas.
- Make changes that make sense to you.
- Listen when others read their work.
- Tell what you like about their work.
- Give only helpful ideas.

The Beach

by Kristi Jones

> Use sense words to tell us about the picnic.

Last week I went to the beach with my family. First, we made sand castles. Then we had a picnic for lunch.

> I really like this line! I can feel the scrunch.

Later, we played on the beach. We threw a ball back and forth. My feet went scrunch on the sand.

> We know you aren't really a shark, so you don't need this part!

Finally, we went swimming. I pretended I was a shark. I wasn't really a shark, though. Then we went home.

Tips for Helping One Another

Sharing your writing with a partner can help you with the writing process. Here are some ways partners can help one another during the writing process.

Talk

- Partners can talk about topics and details. Talking can help you think of ideas.

Listen and Ask

- Partners can listen to or read a first draft. Partners ask questions and make suggestions to help revise the writing.

Check

- Partners can help check writing for conventions. They can help you find and fix mistakes.

Read

- Partners can read and enjoy a final copy. Presenting your writing so that it can be read is one way to publish.

Using the Internet

Using the Internet is a great way to find information. You can search for websites to answer your questions or help with a report.

- A search engine will help you find websites about a topic.
- Many websites tell about an idea, person, place, or thing. If you are not sure whether a website you find is a good source, ask your teacher or parent.
- Write down your sources. Be sure to write the address of the website and the title.

Parts of a Website

URL/
Address
Line

Title

File   Edit   View   Favorites   Tools   Help

Address   http://www.---.org

KIDS CAN HELP!

School kids everywhere CAN help others.
Kids from around the world are joining hands to help others. Kids can—
- hold sales
- build things
- help out
- read to others
- visit hospitals
- put on shows
- write letters

What can you do to help? Visit us!

Websites can link you to people and places around the world. They can help you learn more about a topic. For example, a zoo website might have interesting facts about tigers.

A website for a flower store might have information about roses.

These links can take you to pages with more information.

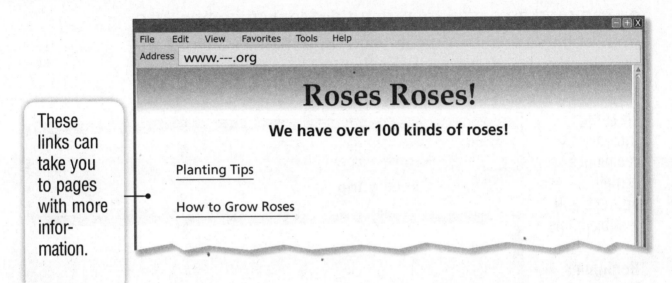

A website about outdoor fun might tell you things to do in the snow.

Websites can also show lists and photos.

Writing for the Web

There are many ways to use technology to write. One way is to write for the Web.

✎ E-mail

You can send an e-mail to a friend or family member. An e-mail is like a letter. You can send an e-mail to anyone in the world if they have an e-mail address, too.

Heading
Includes the recipient's e-mail address and a subject line

Beginning
Tells why you are writing

Middle
Gives details

Ending
Wraps up the message

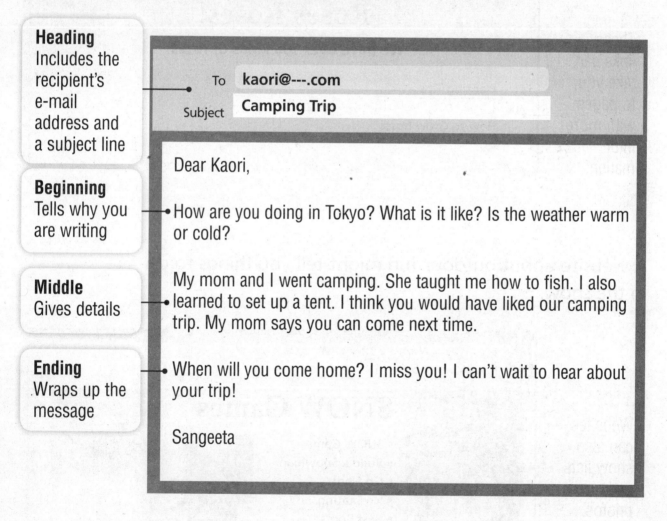

To   kaori@---.com

Subject   **Camping Trip**

Dear Kaori,

How are you doing in Tokyo? What is it like? Is the weather warm or cold?

My mom and I went camping. She taught me how to fish. I also learned to set up a tent. I think you would have liked our camping trip. My mom says you can come next time.

When will you come home? I miss you! I can't wait to hear about your trip!

Sangeeta

Blog Post

Blog is short for "weblog." It is a journal that you keep on the Internet. Other people can read and comment on it. One way to use a blog is to share your opinions about a subject.

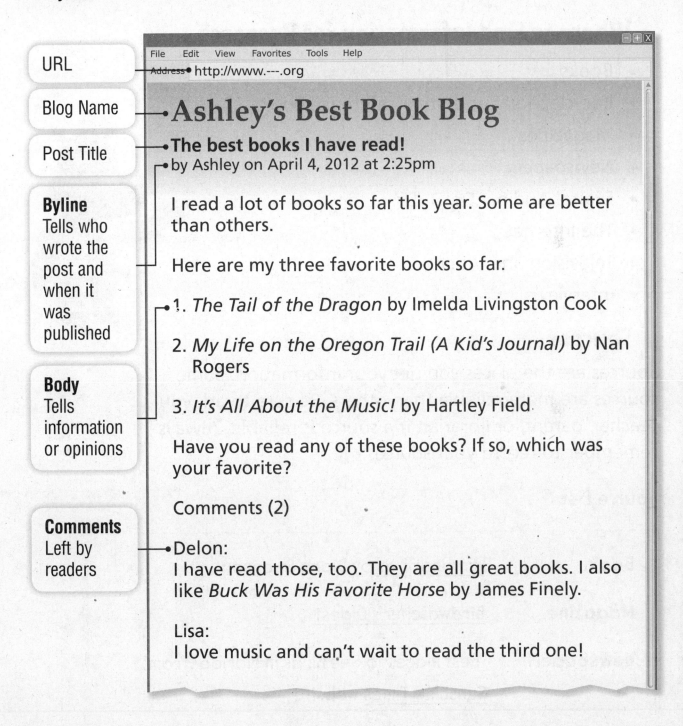

URL

Blog Name

Post Title

Byline
Tells who wrote the post and when it was published

Body
Tells information or opinions

Comments
Left by readers

Address • http://www.---.org

Ashley's Best Book Blog

The best books I have read!
by Ashley on April 4, 2012 at 2:25pm

I read a lot of books so far this year. Some are better than others.

Here are my three favorite books so far.

1. *The Tail of the Dragon* by Imelda Livingston Cook

2. *My Life on the Oregon Trail (A Kid's Journal)* by Nan Rogers

3. *It's All About the Music!* by Hartley Field

Have you read any of these books? If so, which was your favorite?

Comments (2)

Delon:
I have read those, too. They are all great books. I also like *Buck Was His Favorite Horse* by James Finely.

Lisa:
I love music and can't wait to read the third one!

Doing Research

The best way to support your informative or persuasive writing is to use facts and details. The best way to find facts and details is to do research.

Where to Find Information for Research

- Books
- Encyclopedias and other reference books
- Magazines
- Newspapers
- Digital Audio, CDs, DVDs
- The Internet
- Television and Videos
- Interviews

Sources

Sources are the places you get your information. Some sources are more reliable than others. Be sure to ask your teacher, parent, or librarian if a source is reliable. Always remember to record your sources.

Source List

Book:	Hummingbirds by Diane Swanson
Magazine:	Birdwatcher's Digest
Newspaper:	"Best Places to See Birds in Florida" from Sunshine Times website

Finding Information in a Library

A library is organized to help you find information. The books in a library are divided into three main sections: Fiction, Nonfiction, and Reference Books.

- **Fiction** includes stories and chapter books.
- **Nonfiction** books have facts about real people, places, and things.
- **Reference** books include encyclopedias, atlases, and dictionaries. These are kept in a special section of the library.

In addition to books, other reference materials may be available in your library.

- **Magazines and Newspapers** are found in the periodicals area.
- **Computers** with a connection to the Internet may be found in your library.
- **Media**, such as DVDs and CDs, may also be found in your library.

Tips: What does a librarian do?
- chooses and organizes the library's books
- helps you find information
- knows where everything is in the library
- helps you with computer searches
- shows you books and stories you might like

Notetaking

You will find a lot of information when you research. One way to keep track and stay organized is to take notes.

✏ Note Cards

You can take notes on your research on note cards. Write a main idea or a research question at the top of the card. Then write details or the answer to your question below. Be sure to include your source.

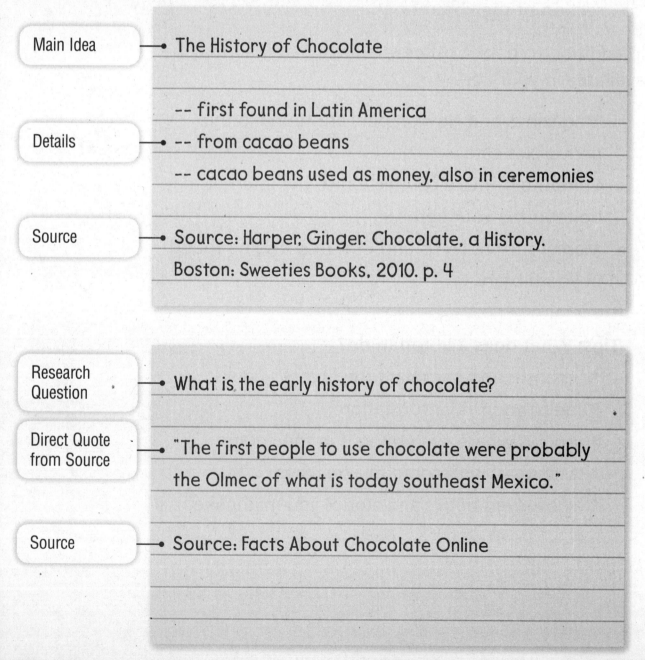

Main Idea ➝ The History of Chocolate

Details ➝
-- first found in Latin America
-- from cacao beans
-- cacao beans used as money, also in ceremonies

Source ➝ Source: Harper, Ginger. Chocolate, a History.
Boston: Sweeties Books, 2010. p. 4

Research Question ➝ What is the early history of chocolate?

Direct Quote from Source ➝ "The first people to use chocolate were probably the Olmec of what is today southeast Mexico."

Source ➝ Source: Facts About Chocolate Online

Interview

When you **interview** someone for research, you ask him or her questions about your topic. Take notes as the person answers your questions.

Interview Tips:

Before the Interview

☐ Think of a person who knows about your topic.

☐ With an adult's help, set up a time to interview this person.

☐ Write questions you would like to ask. Leave space after each to write the answers.

During the Interview

☐ Ask the questions you have prepared.

☐ Listen carefully to the person's answers.

☐ Ask any additional questions that may come up during your interview.

After the Interview

☐ Thank the person for talking with you.

☐ Turn facts from your notes into sentences.

☐ Organize the sentences into paragraphs.

Writing to a Prompt

You may be writing to a prompt in class and on tests. A **prompt** asks a question. When you write to the prompt, answer all parts of the question.

Writing to a Prompt

- Read the prompt carefully. Answer all parts.
- Give details and examples to explain your answer.
- Plan ahead. If the writing is timed, your teacher will tell you when to stop writing.

Written Prompts

A **written prompt** is a statement or question that asks you to complete a writing task. Here is an example of an **informative writing** prompt.

Prompt Asks questions for you to answer	→ Read about the moon. What does it look like? How does it move? Write sentences about the moon.
Details Give facts that answer the first part of the prompt	→ The moon is round. It has light and dark spots. The dark spots are called craters. The
Details Give facts that answer the next part of the prompt.	→ moon moves around Earth. The same side of the moon always faces Earth. The moon may always be round, but the way we see it changes.

Here are some types of written prompts:

Fictional Narrative	Persuasive Writing
These prompts ask you to "tell a story."	These prompts ask you to "convince" or "persuade."
Informative Writing	Response to Literature
These prompts ask you to "tell or explain why."	These prompts ask you to answer questions about a piece you read.

Fictional Narrative Prompt:

Imagine you are an animal.

What type of animal would you be?

Write sentences about what you eat and how you live.

Informative Writing Prompt:

Saturn is a planet in our solar system.

What does Saturn look like?

Write sentences about Saturn.

Response to Literature Prompt:

Think about a character you like from a book you've read.

Describe the character and tell what you like about him or her.

Write sentences about this character.

Checklists and Rubrics

A **rubric** is a chart that helps you when you write and revise. Score 6 tells you what to aim for in your writing.

	• **Focus** • **Support**	• **Organization**
Score 6	My writing is focused. It has facts or details.	My writing has a beginning and an ending. Ideas are in order.
Score 5	My writing is mostly focused. It has facts or details.	My writing has a beginning and an ending. Most ideas are in order.
Score 4	My writing is mostly focused. It has some facts or details.	My writing has a beginning and an ending. Some ideas are in order.
Score 3	Some of my writing is focused. It has some facts or details.	My writing might have a beginning and an ending. Some ideas are in order.
Score 2	My writing is not focused. It has few facts or details.	My writing might be missing a beginning or an ending. Few ideas are in order.
Score 1	My writing is not focused. It has no facts or details.	My writing is missing a beginning or an ending. Few or no ideas are in order.

Circle a number in each row to rate your work.
Then revise your writing to improve your score.

• **Word Choice** • **Voice**	• **Conventions** • **Sentence Fluency**
Ideas are connected with words. I use words that describe. My voice connects with the reader.	My writing has no errors in spelling, grammar, capitalization, or punctuation. Sentences have different lengths.
Most ideas are connected with words. I use some words that describe. My voice connects with the reader.	My writing has few errors in spelling, grammar, capitalization, or punctuation. Most sentences have different lengths.
Some ideas are connected with words. I use some words that describe. My voice may connect with the reader.	My writing has some errors in spelling, grammar, capitalization, or punctuation. Some sentences have different lengths.
Some ideas are connected with words. I use few words that describe. My voice may not connect with the reader.	My writing has some errors in spelling, grammar, capitalization, or punctuation. Few sentences have different lengths.
Few ideas are connected with words. I use few words that describe. My voice may not connect with the reader.	My writing has many errors in spelling, grammar, capitalization, or punctuation. Few sentences have different lengths.
Ideas are not connected with words. I use few words that describe. My voice does not connect with the reader.	My writing has many errors in spelling, grammar, capitalization, or punctuation. No sentences have different lengths. Sentences are incomplete.

Sentences About a Picture

A **sentence** tells a complete thought. It begins with a capital letter and ends with an end mark. You can write sentences about pictures you draw.

Parts of Sentences About a Picture

- A drawing of your own
- Three or four sentences that tell about the picture

Picture
Choose an idea. Draw a picture that shows your idea.

Sentences
Write sentences that tell the main idea of your picture.

This is my cat named Tickles. She loves to play with butterflies. She would never hurt them. Sometimes she bats at them with her paw and then they fly away.

Be sure each sentence
Tells a complete thought. Begins with a capital letter. Ends with an end mark, such as a period or question mark.

Paragraph

A **paragraph** is a group of sentences that tell about one main idea. A paragraph has a topic sentence and detail sentences.

Parts of a Paragraph

- A topic sentence that tells the main idea
- Detail sentences that tell about the main idea
- A first line that is indented

Topic Sentence
Gives the main idea. The first line is indented.

Detail Sentences
Tell about the main idea.

I love when the fair comes to my town. The roller coaster is my favorite ride. **First** we go up and up, and **then** we fly down to the bottom. We even go upside down. Everyone laughs and screams. I was scared the first time I rode the roller coaster. **Now** I can't wait. I love playing all the games, too. **Last year** I won the ring toss game. My prize was a huge stuffed lion that stays on my bed. Soon the fair will be coming again. Maybe I will win a dinosaur this time.

Other Transitions
Second
Next
After that
During
After a while
Meanwhile
Later
Last

Descriptive Paragraph

A **descriptive paragraph** uses sense words. It tells about a person, place, or thing.

Parts of a Descriptive Paragraph

- A topic sentence that tells what is being described
- Details that tell what you see, hear, feel, smell, and taste
- Words that describe color, shape, and size

Topic Sentence
Tells what is being described

Details help you picture what is described.

Sense words tell about sights, sounds, feelings, smells, and tastes.

I love the circus. No matter where I look, there is something fun to see. When I look up, I see trapeze artists. Three of them fly through the air. The crowd cheers. Down on the floor there are three rings. Something different is happening in each ring. In one, furry black bears ride bicycles. One bear stands on his head while he rides around and around. The middle ring has clowns. They have red noses and feet shaped like bananas. They run and tumble. In the third ring, elephants walk slowly. When the trainer claps, they sit on their back legs. Elephants look pretty silly sitting like that. Suddenly I smell something tasty and salty. Peanuts! Yum! Mom buys three bags.

Other Color, Shape, and Size Words
green
square
gigantic
small
round

This topic sentence begins with an interesting description.

My dog Marlo is the best. His fur is soft and brown, but his paws are white. He looks like he's wearing socks. His ears are floppy. One ear looks longer than the other. Marlo's legs are pretty short, but he can run fast. He loves to play catch. You wouldn't believe how high he can jump, even though he's a little guy. Marlo plays hard, but he sleeps hard, too. Marlo will only sleep with me. Dad had to build special pet steps so Marlo could climb onto my bed. Once he's asleep, he doesn't move all night. The next morning, he's ready to run and play all over again. I don't know what I would do without Marlo. I have human friends, but Marlo is my very best friend of all.

Ending Ties the paragraph together

Note how the authors of these descriptions:

- Introduced the topic at the beginning.

  I love the circus. No matter where I look, there is something fun to see.

  My dog Marlo is the best.

- Described many senses, not just sight.

  The crowd cheers.

  Suddenly I smell something tasty and salty.

Summary

A **summary** uses your own words to tell the main ideas or events in a story.

Parts of a Summary

- A beginning that tells the title of the story
- A short retelling of the plot, characters, and setting in your own words
- The most important details or events from the story or article
- Events told in the order in which they happen

Beginning
Gives the name of the story and tells what it is about

Middle
Gives details that tell about the characters, plot, and setting

Details tell the most important events in the order they happen

Summary of *Teacher's Pets*

Teacher's Pets is a story by Dayle Ann Dodds. It is a story about a class and their pets.

In the story, Miss Fry lets her students bring their pets to class. First, Winston brings his pet rooster, Red. He leaves Red behind, so Miss Fry feeds him. The next day, Winston asks if he can leave Red in the classroom for a while. Miss Fry says yes.

Next, Patrick brings his pet tarantula and leaves him in the classroom, too. Then Roger brings in his cricket, Moe. Then all the students bring their pets.

Other Transitions
First
Next
After that
During
After a while
Meanwhile
Later
Last

Miss Fry takes care of the pets after the children leave. She talks to the pets and they do tricks for her. After a while, the whole school can hear the very noisy pets! On Parents' Night, all the mothers and fathers think it is great that Miss Fry likes pets so much.

At the end of the year, all the children take their pets home. But one pet is left behind. Roger leaves his pet cricket Moe. He leaves a note for Miss Fry saying that Moe likes Miss Fry best. Miss Fry brings the cricket home and makes him her pet.

Ending
Tells how the story ends

Note how the author of this piece:

- Chose the important events from the story. The writer didn't include everything that happened in the story but instead chose the most important parts.

- Used her own words. She did not copy the original story. She also used present tense.

Original: On Parents' Night, the mothers and fathers walked around the classroom with great big smiles on their faces. "Isn't it great," they said, "that Miss Fry loves pets so?"

Summary: On Parents' Night, all the mothers and fathers think it is great that Miss Fry likes pets so much.

News Story

In a **news story,** a reporter shares information about a current event. A news story tells who, what, when, where, why, and sometimes how.

Parts of a News Story

- An introduction that tells the topic
- A body that gives details about the topic
- A conclusion that gives one final thought

A **5 W's chart** is a good way to organize information for your news story. It helps you to think about the questions: Who? What? When? Where? Why?

Who is the story about?

What happened?

When did it happen?

Where did it happen?

Why did it happen?

5 W's Chart

Who?	What?	When?	Where?	Why?
New student, Mira Ito	Joined our class	Last week	Room 121	Mira and her family moved to our town.

Now, you can use the information to write your story.

Give your news story a headline, or title.

Introduction
Tells what the topic is

Body
Provides details about the topic

Conclusion
Includes one final thought

New Student in Room 121

Last week, a new student joined our class in Room 121. Her name is Mira Ito. She came all the way from Japan. Mira and her family are American, but her dad's job was in Japan. Last month, Mira and her family moved to our town.

Mira likes to play soccer. Her favorite subjects are math and science. She also plays the violin. She has been taking violin lessons since she was three. Mira has a brother, Ken, and a sister Suzi.

In Japan, Mira had many good friends. She misses them. But she hopes to make new friends here at Woodrow Wilson Elementary School. So stop by Room 121, and say hello to our new friend Mira Ito.

Note how the author of this piece:

- Answered all of the 5Ws questions.

Who?	a new student
What?	joined our class
When?	last week
Where?	Room 121
Why?	her family moved to our town

- Added plenty of interesting details.

Writing for Science

A **science report** gives facts about animals, plants, nature, and other topics in science. It can tell about how something works or explain why it happens.

Parts of a Science Report

- A topic sentence that states the main idea
- Details that support the main idea
- Facts that are correct
- A closing that ties ideas together

Topic Sentence
Tells the main idea or what the paragraph is about

Supporting Details
Give facts about the topic

Ending
Ties ideas together

There are three kinds of honeybees. They all live together in hives. Sometimes there can be thousands of bees living in one hive. There is only one queen bee in a hive. She never leaves. She is much bigger than all the other bees. Her job is to lay eggs. The male bees are called drones. Their job is to make sure there are always enough bees in the hive. The smallest bees are the worker bees. Worker bees are female. They have a stinger and use it when something is bothering them. Some worker bees collect nectar from flowers and bring it back to the nest. Other worker bees make honey from the nectar. One thing is certain. The life of honeybees is very busy.

Other Transitions
First
Next
Often
At times
Sometimes

Writing for Math

A **shape riddle** is usually written about math. It asks you to guess a real life object that has a certain shape.

Parts of a Shape Riddle

- A **topic sentence** that names the shape
- **Body sentences** that give clues to the answer
- A **closing** that asks the riddle question

Topic Sentence
Names the shape

Body Sentences
Give clues and hints to the answer

Closing
Asks the riddle question

What Am I?

I am always a sphere. When you look at me, though, I sometimes look like a circle or a half circle. Sometimes I even look like a backwards letter C or a white banana. I am very big. In fact, I am huge. I cannot fit in your house or in your neighborhood park. I have dark spots and light spots. I have nothing to do with cheese, even though some people think I do. I am certainly not green. No one lives on or near me, but I have been visited. Maybe you will visit me someday, too. What am I?

Answer: The moon.

Other Shapes
cube
cone
cylinder
rectangular prism
pyramid
square
circle
triangle

Paragraph That Explains

A **paragraph that explains** tells how something works or how to do something. It has a topic sentence, body sentences about the topic, and a closing.

Parts of a Paragraph That Explains

- A topic sentence that introduces what the writing is about
- Body sentences that tell about the topic
- A closing that ties ideas together

Topic Sentence
Introduces the main idea

Body Sentences
Give details about the topic

Closing
Ties ideas together

Tag is a great game to play. You can run fast with friends, and the rules are easy. You need at least three people to play. **First,** choose a safe place to play, like a gym or backyard. **Then,** pick a person to be "it." This is the person who will chase everyone. **Next,** the person who is "it" counts to three. Everyone else runs away! **Finally,** the person who gets tagged is the next "it." You can keep playing as long as you want. Tag is my favorite game to play.

Other Transitions
Start
After that
During
After a while
Meanwhile
Later
Last

Recipe

A **recipe** usually tells how to make something to eat. Cookbooks are filled with recipes for all kinds of food.

Parts of a Recipe

- Ingredients, or what you need
- Directions in step by step order
- Helpful hints

Ingredient List
Tells what you need

Directions
Tell what to do, step by step

Hints
Make the recipe even better

Yummy Yogurt Sundae

Here is a healthy treat to make on your own.

For 4-6 People

1 quart plain yogurt

a handful of blueberries

a handful of sliced strawberries

1 sliced banana

1 cup of dry cereal

3 tablespoons honey or maple syrup

1. Mix the yogurt and berries in a large bowl.
2. Mix in the banana.
3. Mix in the cereal.
4. Spoon into small cups.
5. Pour on honey or maple syrup.

You can add walnuts and raisins if you like.

Other Recipe Words
Stir
Blend
Pour
Meanwhile
Later
Next

How-to Paragraph

A how-to paragraph tells readers how to make or do something. It includes steps in order.

✏ Parts of a How-to Paragraph

- A list of materials
- All the steps in order
- Time-order words like *first*, *next*, and *last*
- An ending that ties ideas together

Topic sentence tells what you are explaining →	**Watering Plants When You're Away** Plants need lots of water in order to grow. It can be hard to remember to water your plants. Did you know that you can water your plants even when you're not home? I know a good
Details tell what you need →	trick! You'll need thin cotton rope and a glass of water. First, put the glass of water next to your
Steps shown in order →	plant. Next, push one end of the rope into the soil. Last, put the other end of the rope in the water. The water will travel through the rope
Ending ties ideas together →	from the glass to the plant. Then your plants will get watered, even if you are not there to do it!

How to Fly a Kite

Topic sentence tells what the paragraph will be about →

I love to fly kites. You can try it, too. You will need a kite, some string, and a windy day. Find a good place with lots of space for running, too. First, stand so the wind is blowing on your back. Then, hold up your kite. When the wind blows, toss the kite in the air. Next, run and let out some string. Let out more string if the kite goes up. Now you're flying a kite! If the kite crashes, that's okay. Start over and try again. Flying a kite can be really fun!

Steps shown in order →

Closing sentence wraps up the paragraph →

Note how the author of this piece:

- Explains what the paragraph will be about.

  Did you know that you can water your plants even when you're not home?

  I love to fly kites. You can try it, too.

- Used time-order words like first, next, and then to connect the steps.

  First, stand so the wind is blowing on your back. Then, hold up the kite. Next, run and let out some string.

Directions

Directions tell step-by-step how to do something or get somewhere. Directions use time-order words to help tell what to do. You can use a map to show how to get from one place to another.

Parts of Directions

- A topic sentence about the main idea
- A body with sentences that tell directions in order, step-by-step
- A closing sentence that connects with the main idea

Douglas Elementary School: First Floor

Entrance	102 Ms. Lars	Gym Mr. Woods	
Cafeteria	Courtyard		Boys
			Girls
107 Mr. Ortiz	106 Mr. Cho	105 Mrs. Peter	104 Mr. Smith	Office	103 Ms. Han

Topic Sentence
Introduces the subject: going to the gym

Body
Tells step-by-step directions in order

Closing Sentence
Connects with the main idea

It is easy to get from Mrs. Peter's room to the gym. First, you start in Mrs. Peter's room. Next, you go out the door into the hallway. Then you turn right. Keep walking until you come to the office. Then, turn left. Now, walk down the hallway. Pass the courtyard. At the end of the hall, you will see a door. Open the door. Now, you are in the gym!

Note how the author of this piece:

- Put a title on the directions to make sure readers know what the paragraph is for.

  How to Get to the Gym

- Used time-order words like first, next, and then to connect the steps.

  First, you start in Mrs. Peter's room.
  Next, you go out the door into the hallway.
  Then you turn right.

Paragraph That Compares

A **paragraph that compares** tells how things are alike.
The subjects can be people, animals, places, or things.

Parts of a Paragraph That Compares

- A topic sentence that states the main idea
- Details that tell how things are alike
- An ending that ties ideas together

Topic Sentence
Gives the main idea

Detail Sentences
Tell subjects are alike

Ending
Ties ideas together

Dave and I are alike in many ways. Maybe that's why we are best friends. First of all, we are both good at hockey and play on the same team. Second, we both like to ride our bikes in the park. We like to race to see who gets to the playground first. It doesn't matter who wins because we are faster than all the other kids. Third, we are good at reading and math. Sometimes I ask Dave to help me with a math problem. Sometimes he asks me to explain the meaning of a new word. Our teachers say we are good students. Both of us work really hard. Some people think we're brothers. We don't need to be twins or brothers. What matters is that we are BFFs, best friends forever!

Other Transitions
First
Next
After that
During
After a while
Meanwhile
Later
Last

Paragraph That Contrasts

A **paragraph that contrasts** tells how things are different. The subjects can be people, places, or things.

✎ Parts of a Paragraph That Contrasts

- A topic sentence that states the main idea
- Sentences with details that tell how things are different from each other
- An ending that ties ideas together

Topic Sentence
Gives the main idea

Detail Sentences
Tell how subjects are different

Ending
Ties ideas together

The sun and moon are very different from each other. **First of all**, the sun always looks like a circle in the sky. The moon changes its shape a lot. **Second**, the sun is usually a bright yellow color. It lights up everything it shines on. Right before dark, though, it can turn red. Unlike the sun, the moon is almost always pale white. The moon doesn't give very much light. **Before** breakfast when day begins, the sun shines big, yellow beams through my window. "Time to get up and get busy," it seems to say. **At bedtime**, the moon comes up. Its pale beams shine onto my bed like a nightlight. "Pleasant dreams," the moon seems to say.

Other Words that Contrast
On the other hand
Meanwhile
Instead
However
Yet

Research Report

A **research report** uses your own words to give information about a topic.

Parts of a Research Report

- An introduction that tells the main idea—what the report is about
- A body with facts and details about the main idea
- A graph, diagram, or chart, if needed
- A conclusion that sums up the report

Introduction
Tells the main idea—what the report is about

Details tell what the Big Dipper looks like.

Body
Tells facts and details about the main idea

The Big Dipper

Look up at the stars. See if you can find the Big Dipper. It looks like a big soup ladle made out of stars.

Constellations are groups of stars that look like pictures in the sky. The Big Dipper looks like the ladle you use to lift soup out of a pot. It is part of a constellation called Ursa Major.

There are seven stars in the Big Dipper, and each star has a name. The names are Alkaid, Mizar, Alioth, Megrez, Phecda, Merak, and Dubhe.

The Big Dipper is a helpful group of stars. For example, it can help you find the North Star. The stars on the end of the Big Dipper's bowl point to the North Star. The North Star shows which direction is north. The Big Dipper is also helpful for finding another picture in the sky. First, use the Big Dipper to find the North Star. Then look to the left of the North Star. You will see the Little Dipper. The end of its handle is the North Star.

Examples help make a report more interesting.

Some other names for the Big Dipper are the Big Bear, the Saucepan, and the Plough. Many years ago, some called it The Drinking Gourd.

Conclusion Sums up the main idea

The Big Dipper is a very interesting group of stars. It is one of many pictures in the night sky.

Note how the author of this piece:

- Used words to describe the Big Dipper.
  The Big Dipper looks like the ladle that you use to lift soup out of a pot.

- Could have used a diagram. Instead of just describing the Big Dipper, the author might have included a photo or drawing of it. That would help the reader see what the author is describing.

Graphs, Diagrams, and Charts

Graphs, diagrams, and **charts** are pictures that you can use in your reports. They help to make ideas clear.

> This bar graph compares the number of children who like certain kinds of ice cream.

A **bar graph** helps readers to understand numbers. It compares two or more things.

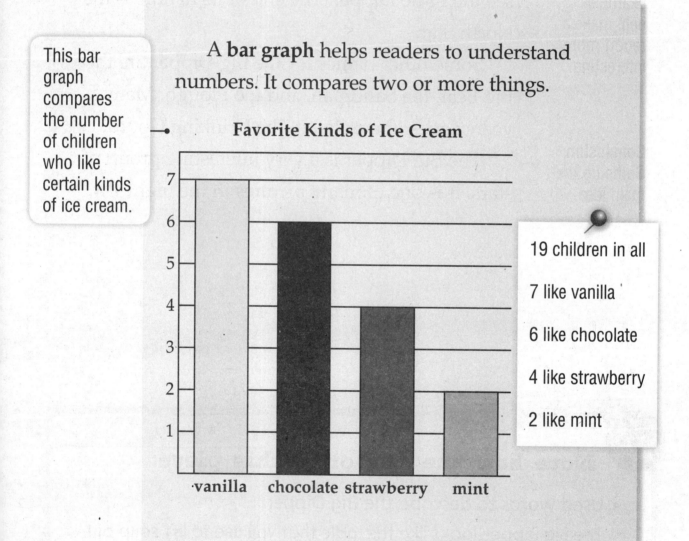

Favorite Kinds of Ice Cream

19 children in all

7 like vanilla

6 like chocolate

4 like strawberry

2 like mint

A **diagram** is a picture that shows how something works or what it looks like.

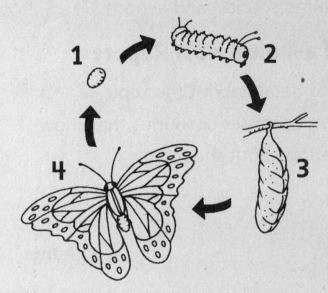

This diagram shows how the lifecycle of a butterfly works.

Labels help readers understand the picture.

A **chart** helps to collect and organize information.

This chart shows the weather for each day of the school week.

This Week's Weather	
Day	Weather
Monday	Sunny
Tuesday	Partly Cloudy
Wednesday	Cloudy
Thursday	Rain
Friday	Rain

Multimedia Report

A **multimedia report** is a presentation of your report that includes pictures, sounds, and actions.

Parts of a Multimedia Report

- Facts and details about the topic
- Slides with pictures or sounds that show information about the topic

	Elephants
A multimedia report begins with a written report.	Elephants are the world's biggest land mammals. They can weigh more than 6 tons. Some grow to be 12 feet tall. An elephant's trunk can be 7 feet long and can weigh 400 pounds.
Each paragraph has one main idea.	An elephant uses its trunk to suck up water. Sometimes it curls its trunk into its mouth to drink the water. Other times it squirts the water over its body to keep cool.

Elephants use sounds to communicate. When elephants are mad, they make a trumpeting sound. When elephants want to say hello to each other, they use low grumbling sounds.

Elephants have few predators because they travel in herds. The main predators are humans. Sometimes, humans hunt and kill elephants for their long, ivory tusks.

Storyboard

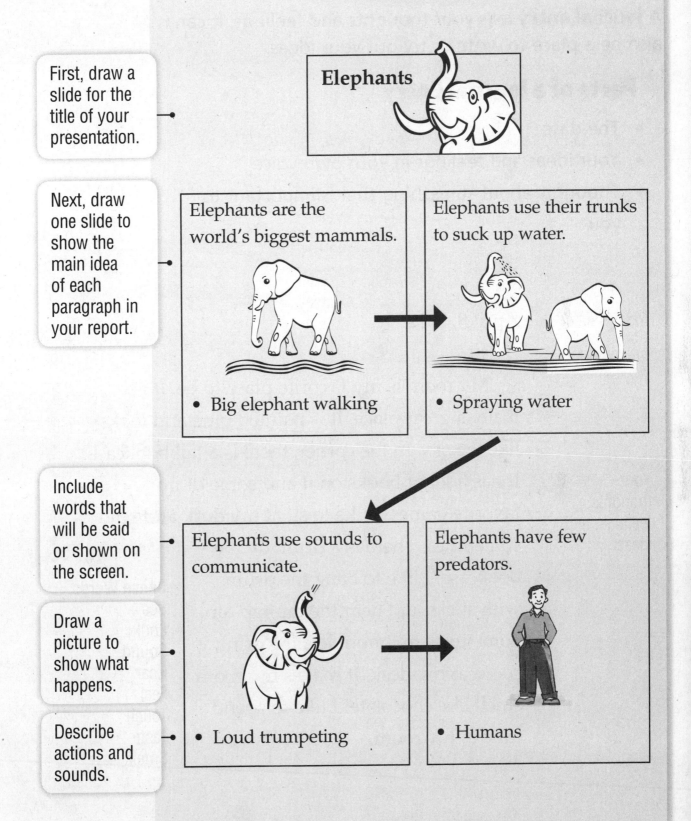

First, draw a slide for the title of your presentation.

Elephants

Next, draw one slide to show the main idea of each paragraph in your report.

Elephants are the world's biggest mammals.

- Big elephant walking

Elephants use their trunks to suck up water.

- Spraying water

Include words that will be said or shown on the screen.

Draw a picture to show what happens.

Describe actions and sounds.

Elephants use sounds to communicate.

- Loud trumpeting

Elephants have few predators.

- Humans

Journal Entry

A **journal entry** tells your thoughts and feelings. It can also be a place to write or try out your ideas.

Parts of a Journal Entry

- The date
- Your ideas and feelings in your own voice
- Thoughts about something that is important to you

Today's date → April 8, 2012

Your thoughts, feelings, and ideas →

My room is my favorite place to be. It is really a great place. It is painted blue and looks like the sky. In the corner, there is a tall bookcase. It has a lot of books on it and some of my favorite games. I like to sit at my desk and read sometimes. There is a drum by the bookcase. I like to bang the drum with sticks and hear the tap-tap-tap. Sometimes my mom lets me drink cocoa at my desk. It makes my room smell like chocolate! I like to spend time in my room.

Sense Words
See
Look
Sound
Hear
Feel
Touch
Taste
Smell

Friendly Letter

A **friendly letter** has five parts. You write a friendly letter to someone you know.

✏ Parts of a Friendly Letter

- The heading (sender's address and date), greeting, body, closing, and signature
- Interesting details
- Your own thoughts and feelings

Heading
With date

Greeting
Whom the letter is to, followed by a comma

Body
Interesting details in your own voice

Closing
Followed by a comma

Signature
Your name

2326 Main Street
Fort Myers, FL 33901
January 7, 2013

Dear Jackson,

    I had the best winter break at my grandparents' house. They live in the mountains. I learned to ski! It was hard at first. When I tried to move on my skis, all I did was fall. I wanted to give up, but Grandma said to keep trying. I tried again and could do it! I skied every day after that. I loved it!

    Grandma and Grandpa said I could bring a friend next time. I hope you can come with me.

        Your friend,

        Elena

Other Transitions
First
Next
After that
During
After a while
Meanwhile
Later
Last

Invitation

An **invitation** is a note or letter that asks someone to do something.

Parts of an Invitation

- The date
- A greeting to the person you are inviting
- A sentence that tells about the event
- Details that give the day, the time, and the place of the event
- A closing and your name

Date	September 3, 2012
Greeting, or the name of the person you are inviting	Dear Jane,
Facts tell about the event and what to bring	You said last week that you really like hiking. Please come with my dad and me on a hike. We plan to visit Fort Cooper State Park. We will go on Saturday, September 12. We will meet at the park gate at 1 o'clock in the afternoon. Be sure to bring good shoes for hiking and a hat for the sun. I know we will have a great time!
Closing and Signature	Your friend, Andrew

Remember to Include
Day
Time
Place
What someone needs to bring

Envelope

An **envelope** is used to send a letter. The **envelope** has to be addressed in a certain way. You will need a stamp from the U.S. Postal Service to send your letter.

Parts of an Envelope

- The return address is in the upper left corner. It gives the name and address of the person who is sending the letter.
- The mailing address is in the middle. It gives the name and address of the person who will get the letter
- A stamp goes in the upper right corner

Return Address
The sender's name and address

Elena Ruiz
2326 Main Street
Fort Myers, FL 33901

Stamp

Mailing Address
Name and address of the person who will get the letter

Jackson Adams
22 Broad Avenue
Miami, Florida 33101

Thank-You Letter

A **thank-you letter** is a short note written to thank someone for doing something nice or giving you a gift.

Parts of a Thank-You Letter

- The sender's address and the date
- A greeting that tells who you are writing to
- A body that tells for what you are thanking someone
- Details that tell your thoughts and feelings
- A closing and your signature

Date

Greeting tells who you are thanking.

Details tell thoughts and feelings.

Closing and Signature

1475 Palm Tree Lane
Pompano Beach, FL 33063
March 8, 2012

Dear Uncle Jack,

Thank you so much for the baseball glove! It was a great gift. Did you know I love baseball? I play on a team in town. I used the glove at a game last week. Also, Dad and I played catch with it. Then I took the glove to the ballpark. We saw my favorite team play. I caught a home run ball! I think this glove is my lucky glove now.

Your nephew,
Adam

Other Closings
Sincerely
Your friend
Love
Regards
Your daughter
Your son

Character Description

A **character description** tells about a person, either real or make-believe. Details paint a word picture that helps readers imagine the character.

Parts of a Character Description

- A topic sentence that tells who the character is
- Body sentences with details about the character
- A closing sentence that tells how the writer feels about the character

Topic Sentence
Introduces the character

Body Sentences
Include details that help readers imagine what the character is like

Closing Sentence
Tells how the writer feels about the character

Grandma Collins is my great-grandma. She always wears white sneakers. She must have a million pairs. Some of them have brightly-colored laces, like hot pink and neon green. Grandma Collins is short and skinny. Sometimes, she likes to wear a bright red hat over her short, white hair. Her face is kind of wrinkly. When Grandma Collins smiles, everyone feels happy. She laughs at almost everything. She must not feel old, because she does lots of things. She rides her bike and plays tennis. She goes on trips to other countries and brings back neat presents. I love Grandma Collins because she is a fun grandma.

Other Describing Words
Big
Wide
Tiny
Wild
Quiet
Soft
Gentle

Personal Narrative

A **personal narrative** is a true story about something that really happened to you.

✏️ Parts of a Personal Narrative

- Words like *I*, *me*, and *my*
- A beginning, a middle, and an ending
- A first sentence that hooks the reader
- Details told in the order they happened

Beginning
The first paragraph makes readers want to know more about the surprise.

This paragraph uses the words *I*, *me*, and *my*.

Dialogue tells what people said.

Middle
The narrator tries to solve the problem.

A Not-So-Nice Surprise

One day last year I found a big surprise in my bedroom. But it wasn't a nice surprise.

Dad picked me up from school that day and we went into the house together. Everything in the house seemed normal to me at first. I was about to go outside and play when I smelled something weird.

"Yuck!" I exclaimed. "What's that smell?"

Dad smelled it too. "I think it's coming from down the hall."

"I'll go check," I said. I walked down the hall. The smell got stronger every time I took a step. Just then, I heard something in my room. It sounded like an animal moving around!

Other Words for *said*
exclaimed
told
yelled
whispered
called
asked
replied

These paragraphs tell details in time order.

This paragraph makes the reader even more curious. What could the animal be?

Ending
The final paragraphs show how the family solved the problem.

I looked in. I saw a black cat with a white stripe sitting on the floor. There was just one problem. We didn't have a cat!

Then the animal looked at me and I saw what it was. It wasn't a cat. It was a skunk!

Dad called a man named Mr. Todd who had a special skunk trap. He trapped the skunk and let it go in the woods. He said I was smart not to try to catch the skunk myself.

We left the window of my bedroom open for two days. We also washed my sheets and blankets—twice! For a while I slept in my sleeping bag on the living room floor. That was cool! But finally the smell was gone! We were glad.

Note how the author of this piece:

- Used details to build suspense.
  Just then, I heard something in my room. It sounded like an animal moving around!

- Gave information about when the event took place.
  One day last year I found a big surprise in my bedroom.

Fictional Narrative

A **fictional narrative** is a made-up story with a setting and a plot. It tells what happens to at least one character.

Parts of a Fictional Narrative

- A beginning, a middle, and an ending
- Events told in time order
- A problem that is solved
- Dialogue, or words spoken by the characters

Beginning
The first paragraph tells the reader about the characters and the setting.

Mr. Morp in Outer Space

Mr. Morp lived in Florida. His favorite thing to do was to fly airplanes. One day he got into his airplane to fly to New Jersey. His friend Dr. Borp came too.

"Can we go to the zoo when we get to New Jersey?" Dr. Borp asked.

Use quotation marks to show that somebody is speaking.

"That would be fun," Mr. Morp said. He turned the steering wheel. "We have to make a left turn here."

Other Action Words
jumped
grabbed
ran
pulled
pushed
opened
stirred

Middle
Shows the problem the characters face.

Suddenly there was a loud beep. They looked out the window. The ground was gone!

"Oh, no!" Dr. Borp said. "Where are we?"

These events are told in time order.

"We must be in outer space," said Mr. Morp.

Dr. Borp pointed to a bright light in front of them. "Is that a star?"

"Yikes!" shouted Mr. Morp. "If we crash into the star it will burn us up!" He turned the steering wheel as fast as he could. The airplane just missed the star. "We are safe!" said Mr. Morp.

"But what's that?" asked Dr. Borp. He pointed again. Now a comet was coming at them!

These paragraphs describe some setting details.

Mr. Morp turned the steering wheel again. The comet whizzed by. "Wow, that was close!" said Mr. Morp.

This part tells about the characters solving the problem.

"I don't want to go to outer space!" Dr. Borp cried. "I want to go home!"

"I'll try to get us home," Mr. Morp told him. He looked at some buttons in front of him. "I think one of these will take us back to Earth."

Dr. Borp wiped his eyes. He saw a red button, a yellow button, and a green button. "The earth has lots of green trees and green grass. So let's try the green button, okay?"

"Okay," said Mr. Morp. He pushed the green button. There was another beep. They looked out the window.

"Look!" said Dr. Borp. "It's the ground!"

"No more stars and comets!" said Mr. Morp. "And look, we're almost to New Jersey!"

Ending
The characters solve the problem

They landed. Then they went to the zoo, and they had a great time!

Fairy Tale

A **fairy tale** is a made-up story that usually includes imaginary creatures or places.

Parts of a Fairy Tale

- A beginning, a middle, and an ending
- A plot that could not really happen
- Some imaginary parts
- Rewards for people who are kind

Beginning
We learn about the main character.

Made-up creatures or places, such as the troll.

Middle
The middle tells us about a problem or conflict.

Details show what the characters are like.

The Troll and His Gold Piece

Once there was a poor farmer. He was digging in his field when he found a gold piece.

"Now I am rich!" he said to himself. "I can buy 100 horses with this money!"

The farmer went home and told his wife. "We are rich!" they said. Then they heard a knock on the door.

An ugly troll was standing on the porch. He had messy hair and he looked angry.

"Where is the gold that you found in the field?" the troll asked. "It is mine."

"No, it is ours," said the farmer.

Other Describing Words
pretty
scary
tall
sad
mean
purple
hungry

"No, it isn't!" said the troll. "My grandmother gave it to me! I want it back NOW!"

"Well, you can't have it!" said the farmer and his wife. They pushed the troll off the porch. Then they went to town to buy horses.

But they dropped the piece of gold along the way. A little girl found it. Her name was Rose. She thought the gold belonged to the troll. So she brought it to him. "Is this your gold?" she asked.

"My gold!" said the troll. "Thank you for bringing it back to me!"

"You're welcome," said Rose.

"Because you were so kind to me, I will give you a reward," said the troll. "I will give you 10 horses!" Poof! There were 10 horses!

"I'm glad I was kind to the troll!" Rose said.

Things didn't go very well for the farmer and his wife. When they got to the market, they chose 10 horses to buy. But when they went to pay, they saw that the gold was gone.

"I can't sell you ten horses if you don't have any gold," said the man at the market.

The farmer and his wife went home without any horses. Rose lived happily ever after.

Ending
Shows how the characters solve the problem.

Play

A **play** is a story that is told in dialogue. It can be performed by actors on a stage.

Parts of a Play

- A beginning, a middle, and an end
- A list of the characters
- Lines that are spoken by the characters
- Stage directions tell what the characters do

The characters in the play are listed here.

The scene is where the story takes place.

The words inside the parentheses are stage directions. They tell what characters do.

Rabbit, Chipmunk, and the Wolves

Characters:

Rabbit

Chipmunk

2 Wolves

Scene: A forest

(*Enter Rabbit and Chipmunk.*)

RABBIT: I just love this forest!

CHIPMUNK: So do I! It's the nicest place I ever lived.

RABBIT: There's plenty of food.

CHIPMUNK: There is lots of sunlight.

(*Wolf 1 and Wolf 2 howl in the distance.*)

RABBIT: Wait—what was that?

CHIPMUNK: I think maybe it was wolf!

RABBIT: It can't be! We don't have any wolves in our forest!

Other Settings for a Play
playground
school
house
sports field
store
sidewalk
desert

Middle
The rabbit and chipmunk have a problem to solve

(*Wolf 1 and Wolf 2 enter.*)

RABBIT: Oh, no! It IS a wolf! Two wolves!

CHIPMUNK: We're in trouble! Hide!

(*Rabbit and Chipmunk hide behind a tree.*)

WOLF 1: What was that noise?

WOLF 2: I think it's rabbits or chipmunks.

The words that each character says are called lines.

WOLF 1: Oh boy! I love to eat rabbits and chipmunks!

CHIPMUNK: What should we do?

RABBIT: I have an idea! Listen!

(*Rabbit whispers to Chipmunk.*)

WOLF 1 (*pointing to tree*): This way!

RABBIT (*in a scary voice*): What was that?

CHIPMUNK (*in a scary voice*): I think it's wolves.

The stage direction shows that Rabbit is speaking in a different voice.

RABBIT (*in a scary voice*): Oh, boy! I love to eat wolves!

WOLF 1: Uh-oh! Did you hear that?

WOLF 2: It sounds big and scary!

WOLF 1: It's probably a monster!

WOLF 2: Let's get out of here! Run!

(*Wolf 1 and Wolf 2 run offstage*)

CHIPMUNK: Yay! We did it!

RABBIT: Great work!

Ending
How the characters solve the problem

CHIPMUNK: I told you that this forest is the nicest place I ever lived!

(*Exit Rabbit and Chipmunk.*)

Poems

A **poem** uses words in a special way to tell about something.

Parts of a Poem

- Details that paint a picture
- Words that use the five senses
- Sometimes rhyming words at the end of lines

Little Green Frog

Details create a word picture

→ Little green frog,

Lies on a log,

Watching the flies,

With his big eyes.

Sense words tell what you see, hear, feel, taste, or smell

→ Buzz in his ear,

The bug is near!

A fat fly goes by,

Frog gives it a try.

Lines that rhyme end with the same sound

→ He sticks out his trap,

His long tongue goes zap!

"Yummy!" says he,

"That's lunch for me."

Rhyming Words
End with same sound
End with same letters

The Snowman

Cold
Snow in the
Yard
We made
A big snowman
With buttons
For eyes
And my old gloves
At the ends of sticks
Were the snowman's
Arms and hands

Details paint a picture for the reader

Note how the author of this piece:

- Chose rhyming words for the first poem.
  Examples: frog/log, flies/eyes, ear/near, trap/zap

- Chose words that appeal to the five senses.
  Examples: green, buzz, long, cold, big, old

Response to Poetry

A **response to poetry** tells what a poem is about and how it makes the writer feel.

Parts of a Response to Poetry

- An introduction that names the poem, its kind, and the author
- A body that tells what the poem is about and the writer's thoughts
- A conclusion that tells how the poem made the writer feel or why the writer liked or disliked the poem

Autumn Fires

In the other gardens
And all up the vale,
From the autumn bonfires
See the smoke trail!

Pleasant summer over
And all the summer flowers,
The red fire blazes,
The grey smoke towers.

Sing a song of seasons!
Something bright in all!
Flowers in the summer,
Fires in the fall!

—*Robert Louis Stevenson*

Introduction
Names the poem and its author

I read a rhyming poem called "Autumn Fires." It was written by Robert Louis Stevenson.

Body
Tells what the poem is about and includes the writer's thoughts about the poem

"Autumn Fires" paints a picture with words. It is about bonfires burning in the fall. I like the part that says, "The red fire blazes, the grey smoke towers." I could almost smell leaves burning and see smoke drifting up into the sky. Some autumn poems are sad, but this one is happy. My favorite part is, "Sing a song of seasons! Something bright in all!" The message of this poem is that there is something special in each season all year long.

Ending
Tells how the poem made the writer feel

I felt cheerful when I read "Autumn Fires." It reminded me of fall days when my dad burns leaves in our backyard.

Fog

The fog comes on
little cat feet.

It sits looking
over harbor and city
on silent haunches
and then moves on.

—*Carl Sandburg*

"Fog" is a poem by Carl Sandburg. It is a free verse poem, so it has no rhyme or pattern.

The poem is short and compares fog to a cat. My favorite part is the beginning. It says, "The fog comes on little cat feet." This means fog comes fast and quietly. It can appear and disappear very fast. The poem also compares fog to a cat sitting quietly.

I like the poem "Fog" because it made me feel quiet and sleepy, like I was wrapped in a soft, fuzzy blanket.

Note how the author of this piece:

- Wrote about the words in the poems and how the words made them feel.

Some other ways to respond to a poem are:

Tell how the poem reminds you of something that happened in your own life.

Draw a picture to go with the poem.

Response to Literature

When you write a **response to literature**, you write about a book you have read. One way to write a response is to compare yourself to a character in a book.

Parts of a Response to Literature

- An introduction that names the book and its author and tells what the book is about
- A body that explains how the writer and the character are alike and different
- A conclusion that tells how the writer feels about the character

Introduction
Tells what the book is about

Body
Tells how the writer and the character are alike and different

This paragraph tells how the writer and character are alike.

Alexander and Me

Alexander and the Terrible, Horrible, No Good, Very Bad Day is a book by Judith Viorst. It is about a boy named Alexander who has a bad day. He thinks that maybe it would be better if he moved to Australia. But his mom says that people in Australia have bad days, too.

Alexander and I are alike because we both have terrible, horrible, no good, very bad days. Some of the things that happened to Alexander have happened to me. For example, I had a cavity when I went to the dentist. I also got in trouble for fighting with my brothers. Alexander

This paragraph tells how the writer and character are different.

and I both hate lima beans, and we have pajamas that we don't like to wear.

Alexander and I are different in a few ways, too. My hair is black, and his is red. I don't chew gum, so I wouldn't get it stuck in my hair like Alexander did. My bad days have one or two bad things happen. Alexander had many bad things happen on his terrible, horrible, no good, very bad day. Also, I do not complain like Alexander. Finally, I wouldn't want to move to Australia. I think I would rather move to Texas.

Conclusion Tells how the writer feels about the character

If Alexander were a real boy, I wouldn't mind being his friend. We could have fun skateboarding together. However, I think all of his complaining might get on my nerves sometimes.

Note how the author of this piece:

- Compared himself to Alexander. To **compare** means to tell how two things are alike.

- Gave examples:
  Some of the things that happened to Alexander have happened to me. For example, I had a cavity when I went to the dentist. I also got in trouble for fighting with my brothers.

Author Review

In an **author review**, the writer tells about books written by one author. The writer also tells his or her thoughts and feelings about the author's books.

✏️ Parts of an Author Review

- An introduction that gives the author's name
- A body that tells about the author's books and why the writer likes them
- A conclusion that sums up the writer's feelings about the author

Introduction
Names the author

Body
Tells about the author's books and why the writer likes them

Cynthia Rylant

Cynthia Rylant is my favorite author. My favorite books by Cynthia Rylant are the ones with Henry and Mudge. There must be a hundred Henry and Mudge books!

Her book <u>Henry and Mudge: The First Book</u> tells how Henry got Mudge. Henry didn't have brothers or sisters. There were no friends on his street. So, he asked his parents for a dog. They said yes! Henry got a puppy named Mudge. Mudge grew into a really big dog. When he licks Henry, it feels gooey and sticky. Cynthia Rylant put a sad part in this book when Mudge gets lost. But, she gave the book a happy ending when Mudge is found. I like her happy endings.

In other Henry and Mudge books, Mudge is grown up. He and Henry have exciting adventures. In <u>Henry and Mudge and the Sneaky Crackers</u>, they are spies. In <u>Henry and Mudge and the Tumbling Trip</u>, they go on a trip to the Wild West. I like these stories because they make me use my imagination.

What I like best about Cynthia Rylant's books are the funny parts. Mudge is so big and playful that he makes messes wherever he goes. For example, in <u>Henry and Mudge and the Bedtime Thumps</u>, Mudge drools all over Grandma's dress, and he accidentally knocks a bowl of peppermints off the table.

Conclusion Sums up the writer's feelings about the author

Cynthia Rylant's books are my favorites because I am an only child like Henry. I have a dog, and he is my best friend. I laugh when I read these books because Cynthia Rylant understands a boy and his dog.

Book Report

A **book report** tells what a book is about without giving away the ending. It names the title, author, and illustrator and includes the writer's feelings about the book.

Parts of a Book Report

- The book title and names of the author and illustrator
- A paragraph that tells about the book
- A paragraph that tells your feelings about the book

Introduction
Names the book's title, author, and illustrator

Body
Tells about the book without giving away the ending

Conclusion
Tells why the writer liked or disliked the book

The Popcorn Dragon

By Jane Thayer

Illustrated by Lisa McCue

A dragon named Dexter liked to blow smoke. He wanted to have friends. The other animals didn't like Dexter because he was always showing off and blowing smoke. Before long, they wouldn't play with Dexter anymore. Dexter felt sad and alone. Then Dexter discovered that he could use his hot breath to do something special.

I liked The Popcorn Dragon because Dexter's friends come back to play with him. I won't tell you why though. You will have to read the story and find out for yourself.

Other Transitions
Soon
After that
Next
Finally
Later
At last

Poster That Persuades

In a **poster that persuades**, a writer uses a picture and a few simple words to show how a problem could be solved.

Parts of a Poster That Persuades

- A topic. What is the problem?
- A picture that makes people think about how the problem could be solved
- A few catchy words about the picture

The top tells the problem.

The picture gives details about the topic.

Catchy words make readers think about the problem and its solution.

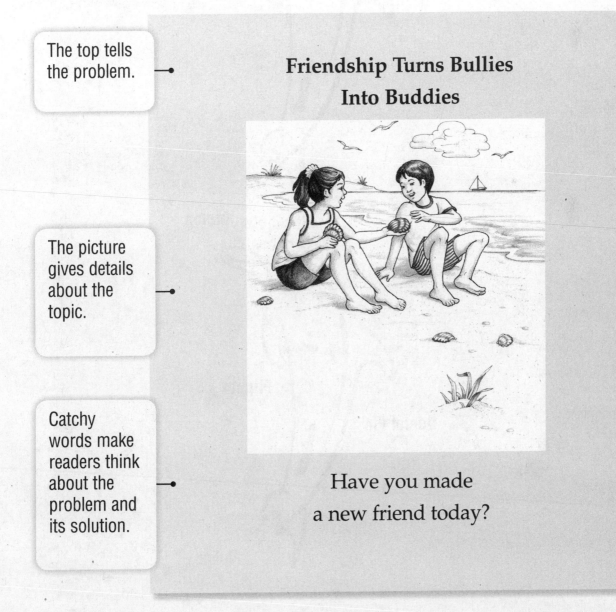

Friendship Turns Bullies
Into Buddies

Have you made
a new friend today?

Labels and Captions

A **label** names a picture. A **caption** tells more about a
picture. A label uses just a few words. A caption includes
one or more complete sentences.

Labels can
be one word
or several
words.

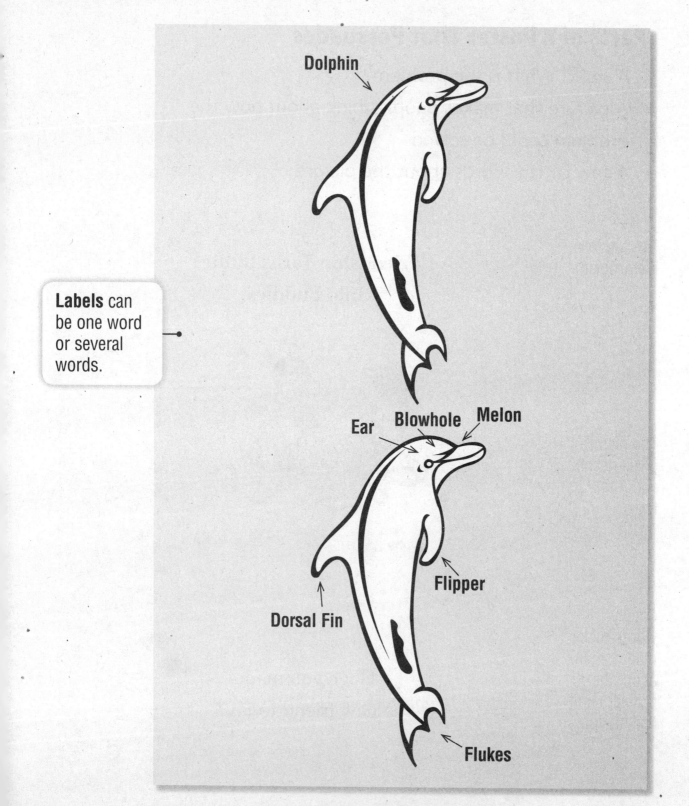

Dolphin

Ear   Blowhole   Melon

Flipper

Dorsal Fin

Flukes

Captions give additional information about a picture.

Bottlenose dolphins live in warm, tropical waters. They can leap up to 16 feet out of the water.

Blowhole

This picture has both a label and a caption.

Bottlenose dolphins breathe through a blowhole near the top of their heads. When dolphins surface, they blow out old air and inhale fresh air.

Notetaking Strategies

Notetaking helps you remember and organize information. Notetaking is helpful when you write a report.

A gathering grid is one way to take notes.

First
Choose a topic. Then, write down two sources where you might find more information about your topic.

Next
Write down three questions about your topic.

Last
Look in your sources for answers to your questions. When you find an answer, write it down in the column under its source.

SUBJECT	SOURCE 1	SOURCE 2
Polar Bear	Encyclopedia	Animal Fact Cards
Where does it live?	The Arctic Circle	Alaska, Russia, Canada, Norway, Greenland
What does it eat?	Seal fat	Ringed and bearded seals
How big is it?	Males, 775-1200 pounds Females, 330-650 pounds	Up to 1,000 pounds

Note cards are another way to take notes.

First
Write one question at the top of the card.

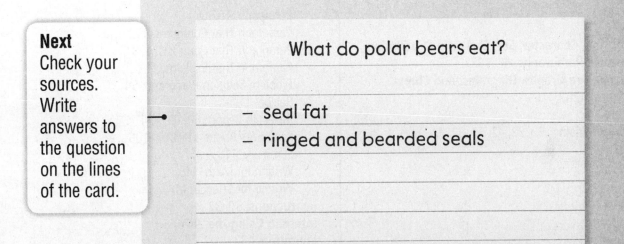

Where do polar bears live?

– in the Arctic Circle
– in Alaska, Russia, Canada, Norway, Greenland

Next
Check your sources. Write answers to the question on the lines of the card.

What do polar bears eat?

– seal fat
– ringed and bearded seals

Add more questions to your gathering grid or note cards. You can use the information to write a report.

Index